100 Bible Games for Everyone

Julia Abrahams

100 Bible Games for Everyone – Julia Abrahams

Order Code: WP745

Copyright: © 2006 Willow Publishing Pty Ltd (ABN 57 097 241 337)
                  PO Box 288 Brookvale NSW 2100 Australia
                  Ph: (02) 9948 3957   Fax: (02) 9948 8153
                  Sales: info@willowconnection.com.au
                  Publishing Enquiries: info@willowpublishing.com.au

This edition published in the United Kingdom by the Bible Reading Fellowship
First Floor, Elsfield Hall, 15-17 Elsfield Way, Oxford OX2 8FG, UK
Tel: 01865 319700 Fax: 01865 319701
Email: enquiries@brf.org.uk

ISBN 1 84101 428 1

ISBN-13 978 1 84101 428 9

First published 2006
10 9 8 7 6 5 4 3 2 1 0

A catalogue record for this book is available from the British Library.

Project Manager: Monica O'Brien
Editor: Tom Raimondo
Assistant Editor: Sue Doggett
Cover Illustration: Graeme Biddle
Graphic Design: Rod Heard

Contents

Section 1
Games Based On Bible Stories

Section 2
Games Based On Christian Living

Section 3
Games Based On Bible Knowledge

Section 4
Games Based On Parables, Proverbs And Images

Section 5
Prayer Games

Section 6
A Game Based On The Theme Of Justice

Introduction

This book contains 100 Bible-based games for both young and mature players. The games for young players are short and straightforward, designed to reinforce a Bible story's meaning. The games for more mature players, including adults, are generally longer and more complex. They may be used to explore a Bible passage or discuss its wider implications.

The games in this book are user-friendly. A Bible verse is given for each game, along with short notes which provide a context. Each game also provides easily accessible introductory notes to assist in choosing the right game for any given time, age, size, setting or preparation constraints. Generally speaking, the preparation required for each game is simple and inexpensive. Many games require no prior preparation.

Each game in this book is categorised by type, such as those based on Bible stories, the parables of Jesus, or Christian living. For games which fall within several categories, a cross-referencing system is provided, along with a number of indices which further sort the games according to Bible reference and age range.

Whether you are working with young children, teenagers or family groups of all ages, you will find this book a very useful tool and a valuable addition to your ministry. Games are a wonderful and enjoyable way to explore Bible stories and themes. They can function as icebreakers, entertaining activities or educational tools. They inspire creative thinking and help us explore life in a way that discursive thought does not. Games are fun!

It is my hope that you will use this book over and over again, and enjoy many hours absorbed in the wonder of God's word.

How To Use This Book

In order to choose a game appropriate for your players and situation, begin by looking at the table of contents. Here, games are listed according to topic. Find a game that appeals to you, and read its introductory notes. These will provide a brief background to the game and help you decide its suitability. In general, all games have a competitive or team element, except the games in Section 1. These games are mostly fun activities for younger players.

If the game seems appropriate, read through its instructions with your group in mind. It is important to consider any special circumstances or needs that may apply to your players. For example, a given game may be intended for children aged three to seven years, yet in your group there are some children who have the maturity and ability of nine year olds. In this case, a game intended for an older age range may be a better choice. In addition, a given game may indicate that it can be played with up to twenty players. If you have a large space and several helpers, you may find that such a game will work with forty players divided into two groups.

Once you have selected a suitable game and before the game begins, it is advisable that you read to the players the Bible passage on which it is based. Older players may read the Bible passage for themselves. This will introduce them to the Bible characters, themes or principles involved within their proper contexts.

The Bible passages quoted in this book are taken from the New International Version (NIV) or the Contemporary English Version (CEV). If you prefer to use a different translation of the Bible, it is advisable to compare the quoted passage with the alternate translation. Some games make use of specific words in the quoted passage, so some slight variations to the game may be necessary if you are using another translation.

Julia Abrahams.

1 Get Up And Walk

Bible verse: "Get up... and go home!" Matthew 9:6.

Setting: Indoors or outdoors.
Number of players: Up to 20. Divide larger numbers into smaller groups.
Time: 5-10 minutes.
Preparation: None required.
Age: 3-7 years.

This game and the following game are based on a story from the Gospel of Matthew, in which Jesus shows his power and his love by curing a man who could not walk.

Ask the players to sit in a circle. Tell them that while they sit in the circle, they cannot walk. Then, select one player to stand up. Tell everyone that this player represents Jesus. Jesus can walk. Jesus can also make others walk by tapping them on the shoulder and saying, "Get up and go home".

Begin the game by asking Jesus to walk around the circle, tapping each player on the shoulder. When Jesus taps a player on the shoulder and says "Get up and go home", the two must run around the circle in opposite directions, as fast as they can. They must then attempt to be the first to sit down in the circle. The first to sit down becomes one of the players who cannot walk, and the other becomes Jesus. The game may then be repeated as often as desired.

2 Musical Get Up And Walk

Bible verse: "Get up... and go home!" Matthew 9:6.

Setting: Indoors or outdoors.
Number of players: Up to 20. Divide larger numbers into smaller groups.
Time: 5-10 minutes.
Preparation: A CD or cassette player and a Christian music recording are required.
Age: 3-7 years.

This game is a variation of Get Up And Walk (Game 1).

The game is played as described above, except that the player who will race in the opposite direction to Jesus around the circle is selected when the music stops.

As the music is playing, ask Jesus to walk around the outside of the circle, tapping each player on the shoulder. When the music stops, Jesus says, "Get up and go home", and the last player to be touched on the shoulder races Jesus around the circle. The first to sit down becomes one of the players who cannot walk, and the other becomes Jesus.

3 Follow Me In A Circle

Bible verse: "Come, follow me." Mark 1:17.

Setting: Indoors or outdoors.
Number of players: Any number.
Time: 5-10 minutes.
Preparation: None required.
Age: 3-7 years.

This game is based on a passage from the Gospel of Mark, in which Jesus calls Simon and Andrew to come and follow him. It introduces the players to the concept of discipleship by allowing them to observe and then follow the example of others.

Ask the players to sit or stand in a circle, and select one to represent Jesus. Instruct this player to say, "Follow me", and invent an action, such as clapping hands, stamping feet or waving arms. The other players must copy this action.

After about a minute has elapsed, ask another player to represent Jesus. Invite this player to invent a different action for everyone to copy. The game continues until all players have had the opportunity to represent Jesus.

4 Follow Me In A Line

Bible verse: "Come, follow me." Mark 1:17.

Setting: Indoors or outdoors.
Number of players: Any number.
Time: 5-10 minutes.
Preparation: None required.
Age: 3-7 years.

This game is a variation of Follow Me In A Circle (Game 3).

The game is played as described above, except that instead of sitting in a circle, the players form a line at the beginning of the game. The player representing Jesus stands at the head of the line.

To begin the game, Jesus says, "Follow me", and moves forward by jumping, skipping, running, hopping and so on. The other players then copy this action. After about a minute has elapsed, the leader moves to the back of the line, and the next player becomes Jesus. Instruct this player to invent a new action for everyone to copy.

5 Naaman Is Well Again

Bible verse: "So he went down and dipped himself in the Jordan seven times." 2 Kings 5:14.

Setting: Outdoors.
Number of players: Any number.
Time: 5-10 minutes.
Preparation: A sprinkler or hose is required.
Age: 3-7 years.

This game is based on the story of Naaman, a valiant army commander. Naaman has leprosy, and is instructed by the prophet Elisha to bathe seven times in the River Jordan to be cured. Namaan trusts Elisha and does as he is told. After he has bathed seven times, Namann is well again.

This game is ideal for a very hot day. Tell the players that they are going to act out Naaman's story. Tell them that the hose or sprinkler represents the River Jordan, and that they will run through it seven times, just like Naaman.

Ask the players how Naaman would have felt when he was well again. They will probably tell you that he felt happy. Tell the players that they will also feel happy when they have run through the hose or sprinkler. Invite them to shout and sing as they do this, remembering how happy Naaman was when he was cured by God.

6 Escape To Egypt

Bible verse: "Escape to Egypt." Matthew 2:13.

Setting: Indoors or outdoors.
Number of players: Up to 30.
Time: 5-10 minutes.
Preparation: None required.
Age: 3-7 years.

This game is based on the infancy narrative from the Gospel of Matthew. In this story, an angel appears to Joseph in a dream and warns him that King Herod wants to hurt baby Jesus. The angel instructs Joseph to take baby Jesus and Mary to safety in Egypt. Ask the players to sit in a circle and be very still. Tell them that when they hear the words, "Escape to Egypt!", they must stand up and run away as fast as they can. Then, when they hear the word, "Egypt!", they must reform the circle and sit down. This game may then be repeated as often as desired.

7 Fishers

Bible verse: "And I will make you fishers of men and women." Matthew 4:19.

Setting: Indoors or outdoors.
Number of players: Up to 20. Divide larger numbers into smaller groups.
Time: 5-10 minutes.
Preparation: A packet of balloons, a permanent marker and a bed sheet or large cloth are required.
Age: 3-7 years.

This game is based on a passage from the Gospel of Matthew, in which Jesus tells Simon Peter and Andrew that he will make them fishers of men and women. This statement does not apply to Simon Peter and Andrew alone. As disciples of Jesus, we are also called to share his love with everyone we meet.

Using a permanent marker, draw a small fish shape on each balloon. It is easiest to do this before blowing the balloon up. Then, place all the inflated balloons on the bed sheet or large cloth, and ask four players to each hold a corner.

Instruct the players to stand around the bed sheet. To begin the game, say the following rhyme with them:

Catch the fish!
Catch the fish!
Catch the fish,
as many as you wish!

On the last word of the rhyme, instruct the four holders to lift the sheet up so that the balloons fly into the air. The players, including the holders, must then run around trying to catch as many balloons as possible.

8 Balaam's Donkey

Bible verse: "When the donkey saw the angel standing there with a sword, it walked off the road and into an open field." Numbers 22:23.(CEV)

Setting: Indoors or outdoors.
Number of players: Up to 20.
Time: 5-10 minutes.
Preparation: A cardboard or plastic sword is required.
Age: 3-7 years.

The story of Balaam and his donkey is found in the Book of Numbers. Balaam and his donkey are on a journey. The angel of the Lord appears at various times with a drawn sword to keep them from danger. Unlike Balaam, the donkey is able to see the angel, and it turns aside to keep Balaam safe. Balaam does not understand why the donkey changes direction and becomes very cross. The angel and the donkey speak to Balaam, and he finally understands.

Select one player to represent the angel. Give this player the sword, and ask him or her to stand in the centre of the space. Tell the other players that they represent Balaam's donkeys, and ask them to stand in a circle around the angel. Tell them that they are on a journey which has many dangers, but the angel of the Lord will keep them safe. Instruct the players to watch the angel of the Lord very carefully, because the angel will only be able to direct them with actions, not words. It will show them a safe path by gesturing with the sword.

The angel may make the following gestures:

1. Hold the sword behind his or her back: it is safe for the donkeys to go forward.
2. Hold the sword out in front: the donkeys must stop.
3. Point the sword towards the floor: the donkeys must crouch down.
4. Point the sword to the left or right: the donkeys must go left or right.

You may wish to practise these gestures and their meaning with the players before you begin.

The angel starts the game with the sword behind his or her back. The players then gallop around the circle, and the angel occasionally makes a different gesture with the sword. The players must watch the gestures carefully and perform their accompanying actions. Any player that does not observe the gestures must leave the game. The last player left is the winner, and becomes the angel when the game repeats.

9 God Made The World

> **Bible verse:** "In the beginning, God created the heavens and the earth." Genesis 1:1.

Setting: Indoors or outdoors. A large space is required.
Number of players: Any number.
Time: 5-10 minutes.
Preparation: A CD or cassette player and some atmospheric music are required.
Age: 3-7 years.

This game is based on the first chapter of Genesis, which describes the creation of the heavens and the earth. It explores the concept of the right order of creation and the belief that God created and sustains all things.

To begin the game, play the CD or cassette of atmospheric music. Tell the players that you are going to read them a story about the creation of the world. As you read the story, ask them to imagine the places, animals and people that are described. Then, invite them to act out the various things that God has made.

Slowly read the following story to the players, pausing between each phrase so as to allow enough time for them to act out the parts of Creation.

In the beginning, God said, "Let there be light," and there was light. There was night and there was day.

God said, "Let there be waters," and there were big oceans and seas.
God said, "Let there be ground," and there was solid earth.
God said, "Let there be sky," and there was sky.
God said, "Let there be little seeds to grow and grow into beautiful flowers and big trees, spreading their branches everywhere."
God said, "Let there be twinkling stars in the sky, with the bright beautiful sun and the shining moon."
God said, "Let there be fish swimming in the seas. Let there be snakes, spiders, lizards and insects crawling on the ground. Let there be birds and butterflies flying through the air. Let there be animals that run and gallop and jump. Let there be animals that grunt and growl and howl. Let there be animals as quiet as a mouse."

Last of all, God said, "Let there be human beings, men and women, boys and girls."

God made all of these. God saw that they were good.

10 Jacob's Ladder

Bible verse: "He had a dream in which he saw a stairway resting on the earth, with its top reaching to heaven, and the angels of God were ascending and descending on it." Genesis 28:12.

Setting: Indoors or outdoors. A large space is required.
Number of players: Up to 20. Divide larger numbers into smaller groups.
Time: 5-10 minutes.
Preparation: Twenty sticks or pieces of rope are required.
Age: 3-7 years.

This game is based on a passage from Genesis which records Jacob's amazing dream. Jacob dreams of a ladder between heaven and earth on which the angels ascended and descended. It is designed to reinforce Bible knowledge.

To prepare for this game, arrange the sticks or pieces of rope in a long row, about a metre apart. Tell the players that this represents the ladder that the angels climbed up and down.

To begin the game, tell the players that they are going to climb the ladder, just like the angels. To do this, they will need to jump between each stick or plank on the way up and the way down. Instruct the players to form a line, and one by one, climb the ladder both up and down.

11 Jesus Calms The Storm

Bible verse: "He got up and rebuked the winds and the waves, and it was completely calm." Matthew 8:26.

Setting: Indoors.
Number of players: Up to 20.
Time: 10-15 minutes.
Preparation: Two large sheets and a long rope are required.
Age: 3-7 years.

In this game the players act out the story of Jesus saving his disciples from the storm. Help the players to visualise the story by varying the pitch and tone of your voice as you describe the height of the waves and the ferocity of the wind that batter the disciples' boat.

Lay the rope on the floor in the shape of a boat, and place a sheet on each of its sides. Then, invite the players to step inside the boat. Select one player to represent Jesus. Ask this player to pretend to be asleep. Select eight other players to represent the wind and waves. Invite them to step outside the boat and each take a corner of the sheets. Tell the remaining players that they represent Jesus' disciples.

Begin the game by telling the disciples that they are on a journey with Jesus. Then, instruct the players outside the boat to flap their sheets in imitation of a huge storm. When the disciples are ready, they may ask Jesus for help. Jesus may help them immediately, or remain asleep until they ask again. Then Jesus must say, "Be still!" to the winds and waves, which die down immediately.

The players may then change their roles in the game as many times as desired.

12 Moses In The Basket

> *Bible verse:* "When she could hide him no longer, she got a papyrus basket…(and) placed the child in it." Exodus 2:3.

Setting: Indoors or outdoors. A space with a number of hiding places is required.
Number of players: Up to 20. Divide larger numbers into smallergroups.
Time: Up to 15 minutes.
Preparation: A basket and a baby doll are required.
Age: 3-7 years.

This game is based on the story of Moses' early life. As an infant, Moses is in great danger because the Pharaoh has ordered that all Hebrew boys must be killed. His mother saves him by placing him in a wicker basket and hiding him in the reeds on the River Nile. Having escaped this danger, Moses faces drowning or starvation. He is saved by the Pharaoh's daughter, who finds him in the reeds and adopts him. In both of these actions, we see God's providence.

Place the baby doll in the basket. Tell the players that the doll represents Moses. Tell them that Moses is not safe, and that his mother is going to hide him from danger.

Select a player to represent Moses' mother. Ask the other players to leave the room and allow Moses' mother time to hide the basket. When this is done, instruct Moses' mother to say, "The baby is hidden". The players may then enter the room and try to find the baby in the basket.

The player who finds the baby becomes the Pharaoh's daughter, the Princess. The Princess may choose a player to have the next turn at representing Moses' mother, and the game repeats.

13 A Star Was A-Shining

Bible verse: "We saw his star in the east." Matthew 2:2.

Setting: Indoors.
Number of players: Any number.
Time: 5-10 minutes.
Preparation: None required.
Age: 3-7 years.

This game is very appropriate for the Christmas season. It is based on the infancy narratives from the Gospels of Matthew and Luke. The story of the star and the wise men can be found in Matthew 2:1-12, while the shepherds and angels appear in Luke 2:8-20.

Ask the players to stand in a circle. Tell them that you are going to say a rhyme together, and ask them to copy your actions. The rhyme and actions are given below: (Twinkle your fingers high in the air, like a star.)

A star was a-shining, a-shining, a-shining,
A star was a-shining above baby Jesus.

(Wave your arms like an angel.)

Angels were singing and singing and singing,
Angels were singing to greet baby Jesus.

(Hold hands and walk around the circle.)

Shepherds were walking and walking and walking,
Shepherds were walking to see baby Jesus.

(Hold hands and gallop around the circle.)

Wise men were riding and riding and riding,
Wise men were riding to see baby Jesus.

(Rock a baby in your arms.)

Mary was rocking and rocking and rocking,

Mary was rocking the dear baby Jesus.

(Kneel down on one knee.)

Joseph was kneeling and kneeling and kneeling,
Joseph was kneeling before baby Jesus.

14 Over The Sea

Bible verse: "But Jonah ran away...He went down to Joppa, where he found a ship...After paying the fare, he went aboard and sailed for Tarshish." Jonah 1:3.

Setting: Indoors or outdoors. A large space is required.
Number of players: Any number.
Time: Up to 15 minutes.
Preparation: Two ropes are required.
Age: 3-7 years.

This game is based on the Book of Jonah, in which Jonah tries to avoid doing as God asks. Rather than go to Nineveh, he takes a ship bound for Tarshish. However, Jonah soon learns that disobeying God's commands leads to disaster. His trip is interrupted by a mighty storm and he is thrown overboard.

Place the two ropes on the ground, very close together. Tell the players that the space between the ropes represents the sea. Tell them that Jonah tried to cross the sea to escape from God. He did not get very far before there was a big storm and he was thrown into the water.

Ask the players to jump over the sea, one by one. If they succeed in reaching the other side, they may continue until the next round. If they do not reach the other side, they must leave the game. As the game progresses, gradually move the ropes further and further apart, so that the sea gets wider and wider. When a player cannot jump over the sea, ask everyone to say, "Jonah is in the water!" The winner is the last player left in the game.

15 Jonah In The Whale

> **Bible verse:** "But the Lord provided a great fish to swallow Jonah, and Jonah was inside the fish three days and three nights." Jonah 1:17.

Setting: Indoors or outdoors. A large, clearly defined space is required.
Number of players: Any number.
Time: Up to 15 minutes.
Preparation: A large rope and a watch are required.
Age: 3-7 years.

People of all ages love the story of Jonah and the whale. It is full of fun and adventure. It is a story of God's providential love and care for his people.

Lay the rope on the ground in a roughly circular shape. Tell the players that this represents the belly of the whale that swallowed Jonah. Instruct them that the belly of the whale is safe from the huge storm that is raging outside. Select one player to represent the whale, and another to be the timekeeper. Give the timekeeper the watch, and instruct him or her to stop the game after three minutes. Tell the remaining players that they all represent Jonah.

The object of the game is for the whale to catch as many players as possible and put them in the belly. The game begins when the timekeeper shouts out, "Catch Jonah! Keep him safe!" The whale must then run around and touch as many players as possible. Each player who is touched must run and sit in the belly of the whale. At the completion of three minutes, the timekeeper shouts out, "Stop!" to end the game. A new whale and timekeeper may then be selected, and the game repeats.

16 Parting The Red Sea

> **Bible verse:** "And the Israelites went through the sea on dry ground, with a wall of water on their right and on their left." Exodus 14:22.

Setting: Indoors or outdoors.
Number of players: Any number.
Time: Up to 15 minutes.
Preparation: None required.
Age: 3-7 years.

The crossing of the Red Sea is one of the best loved stories from the Old Testament. It tells of God's mighty works and steadfast love for the Israelites.

Divide the players into two equal groups. Ask them to stand in two lines, facing a partner in the opposite line and holding their partner's hands. Tell the players that they represent the waters of the Red Sea, and that no one can cross the Red Sea unless Moses says, "Part the waters!"

Invite the two players at the head of the lines to represent Moses and Aaron. Moses must stand facing the Red Sea, raise his or her hands and shout, "Part the waters!" All the players in the line then raise their hands up high so that Moses and Aaron can run between the lines. However, if Aaron says "Part the waters!" instead of Moses, the players must remain still.

When they reach the end, Moses and Aaron rejoin the lines. All the players then hold hands and the game begins again. The two players at the head of the lines now have the opportunity to play Moses and Aaron, and the game may continue until each player has had a turn at parting the Red Sea.

17 Daniel In The Lion's Den

Bible verse: "My God sent his angel, and he shut the mouth of the lions. They have not hurt me." Daniel 6:22.

Setting: Indoors or outdoors. A large, clearly defined space is required.
Number of players: Up to 20.
Time: Up to 15 minutes.
Preparation: None.
Age: 3-7 years.

Daniel was a good man who trusted in God. When King Darius had him thrown into the lions' den, Daniel prayed and God kept him safe. God sent an angel to save Daniel from the hungry lions.

Divide the players into two groups. Tell the first group that they represent the angels, and ask them to stand on one side of the space. Tell the second group that they represent the lions, and ask them to stand on the other side of the space.

The object of the game is for the angels to stop the mouths of the lions before they have a chance to eat Daniel. They can do this by tapping the lions on the shoulder. Once a lion has been tapped, he or she must leave the game.

Begin the game by shouting, "Go and save Daniel!" At this command, the angels must chase the lions and try to tap them on the shoulder. The game continues until all the lions have been tapped.

18 God's Children

Bible verse: "You are...God's children." Galatians 4:7. (CEV)

Setting: Indoors.
Number of players: Up to 30. Divide larger numbers into smaller groups.
Time: Up to 15 minutes.
Preparation: Tables, play-dough and play-dough models for the children to copy are required.
Age: 3-7 years.

Creativity is one of God's many wonderful attributes. As we are made in God's image, we too enjoy creating things.

In this game, the players celebrate their God-given ability to create by making play-dough models of characters and objects from the Bible.

Begin by reminding the players of a Bible passage which they have heard recently. It is best to choose a story with concrete images, such as a boat, star or donkey. Tell the players that they are going to have fun by making some of these images with play-dough.

To make play-dough, mix two parts plain flour with one part salt. Add one quarter of a teaspoon of oil and a small amount of water. A few drops of food colouring may also be added, if desired. Mix with a wooden spoon or knead with fingers until the mixture has an even consistency. Store the play-dough in an airtight container until required.

19 Hide The Spies

Bible verse: "She had taken them up to the roof and hidden them under the stalks of flax she had laid out on the roof." Joshua 2:6.

Setting: Indoors or outdoors. A space with a number of hiding places is required.
Number of players: Up to 30. Divide larger numbers into smaller groups.
Time: Up to 15 minutes.
Preparation: None required.
Age: 3-7 years.

This game is based on an early section of the Book of Joshua, in which Joshua sends two Israelite spies into Jehrico. The spies are helped by Rahab, who hides them from the king of Jericho under the flax she keeps on the roof of her house.

This is a "hide and seek" game. Select one player to represent the king of Jericho. This player begins the game by facing a wall and counting to twenty. The remaining players, who represent the Israelite spies, take this opportunity to hide.

At the count of twenty, the king of Jericho shouts out, "I'm coming to get you", and proceeds to find all the spies. The last spy to be found is the new king of Jericho.

20 Spread The Word About The Kingdom

Bible verse: "After this, Jesus travelled about from one town and village to another, proclaiming the good news of the kingdom of God." Luke 8:1.

Setting: Indoors or outdoors. A large space is required.
Number of players: Any number.
Time: 5-10 minutes.
Preparation: None required.
Age: 3-7 years.

This game introduces the players to the importance of the kingdom of God. It emphasises the huge amount of time Jesus spent travelling from place to place in order to speak to people about the kingdom, and the variety of ways in which he travelled.

Begin by telling the players that the kingdom of God is very, very important. Jesus spoke about it more than anything else. He travelled from place to place telling people the Good News about God's kingdom and God's great love. However, Jesus didn't have motor cars or aeroplanes. He travelled on foot, on a donkey or in a boat.

Ask the players to stand in a circle. Invite them to show you how they can walk on the spot, pretend to ride a donkey, and pretend to sail a boat. Then, ask them all to face in the same direction.

Tell the players that they are going travel as Jesus did, walking, riding or sailing from place to place to tell people about the kingdom of God. Instruct them that when you say 'walk', they must walk on the spot; when you say 'ride', they must pretend to ride a donkey; and when you say, 'sail', they must pretend to sail a boat.

Start by giving your instructions slowly, and gradually give them faster and faster. Say them in a random order to challenge the players. The game may then continue for as long as desired.

21 We Boarded A Ship

Bible verse: "They sailed to the region of the Gerasenes, which is across the lake from Galilee." Luke 8:26.

Setting: Outdoors.
Number of players: Up to 8. Divide larger numbers into smaller groups.
Time: Up to 15 minutes.
Preparation: A large tub of water and some small paper or plastic cups are required.
Age: 3-7 years.

One of the features of Luke's Gospel is the meaning attached to Jesus' travels across the lake of Galilee. One side of the lake was the territory of the Jews, but the other was not. Through Jesus' visits to these different territories, Luke makes the point that Jesus' mission was not just for the chosen people of the House of Israel, but for all people in this world. We are all God's children.

Tell the players that when Jesus was grown up, he often travelled across the lake of Galilee. He was very busy, talking to the people about God. He wanted to make sure that everyone knew the Good News that God loved them all. Tell them they are going to be like Jesus, and travel across the water so that they can spread the Good News.

To prepare for this game, fill the tub with water. Then, give each player a paper or plastic cup. Tell them that their cup represents a boat. The object of the game is for the players to race their boats across the tub of water by blowing through their mouths. Instruct them to shout, "God loves everyone!" as soon as their boat reaches the other side.

22 Let The Children Come To Me

> **Bible verse:** "Let the little children come to me, and do not hinder them." Luke 18:16.

Setting: Indoors or outdoors. A medium-sized space is required.
Number of players: Up to 20 players.
Time: 5-10 minutes.
Preparation: None required.
Age: 3-7 years.

This game is based on a story from the Gospel of Luke, in which Jesus encourages little children to come to him, even though the disciples try to stop them.

Select one player to represent Jesus, and ask him or her to stand in the centre of the space. Divide the remaining players into two groups. The first group represents the little children, and the second group represents the disciples. Ask the disciples to stand in a small circle around Jesus, and the little children to stand in a wider circle around the disciples.

The game begins when the little children shout, "We want to see Jesus!" The disciples must shout, "No! No!", and beckon for the children to go away. The children then start running towards the disciples, trying to find a way to reach Jesus. The disciples also start running and try to touch the little children. Any child who is touched by a disciple must sit down.

Jesus can end the game by shouting, "Let the little children come to me!" All the children, whether sitting or standing, jump up and run to Jesus, followed by the disciples. The game then repeats, and a new child is selected to represent Jesus.

23 Noah And The Ark

> **Bible verse:** "You are to bring into the ark two of all living creatures, male and female." Genesis 6:19.

Setting: Indoors.
Number of players: Up to 30.
Time: 5-10 minutes.
Preparation: None required.
Age: 3-7 years.

This game is based on the well known story of Noah and the ark.

Ask the players to form a large circle, all facing in the same direction. If there is a large number, you may wish to form two circles. Tell the players that they represent the animals that Noah took into the ark. Tell them that as you call out each animal's name, they are to imitate that animal.

Start the game by saying the following rhyme:

Noah's ark was like a zoo.
The animals came two by two.
There were lots of animals.
Can you guess who?

Then, say the names of a number of animals, such as monkeys, birds, giraffes and sheep. Each time a new animal is mentioned, say the rhyme above. The players will quickly memorise it, and you may say it together.

As a variation of this game, you may wish to ask the players to each nominate an animal to be imitated.

24 Jesus Enters Jerusalem

> *Bible verse:* "When Jesus entered Jerusalem, the whole city was stirred and asked, 'Who is this?'" Matthew 21:10.

Setting: Indoors or outdoors. A medium-sized space is required.
Number of players: Up to 20. Divide larger numbers into smaller groups.
Time: 5-10 minutes.
Preparation: A cloak or sheet and some branches are required.
Age: 3-7 years.

This game is based on the story of Jesus' triumphant entry into Jerusalem.

Select one player to represent Jesus, and wrap him or her in the cloak or sheet. The remaining players represent the people of Jerusalem. Ask them to form two lines, facing each other, and give each player a branch.

To begin the game, ask Jesus to pretend to ride a donkey towards the two lines. As he or she approaches, instruct the people of Jerusalem to shout, "Jesus is coming, Jesus is coming!" When Jesus reaches the beginning of the lines, the people of Jerusalem raise their branches and shout, "Hosanna!", and Jesus gallops forward. When Jesus reaches the end of the lines, the game may repeat. Select a new player to represent Jesus.

25 Zacchaeus In The Tree

> *Bible verse:* "Zacchaeus, come down immediately." Luke 19:5.

Setting: Indoors or outdoors. A medium-sized space with a number of hiding places is required.
Number of players: Up to 20. Divide larger numbers into smaller groups.
Time: 5-10 minutes.
Preparation: None required.
Age: 3-7 years.

This game is based on the story of Jesus' meeting with Zacchaeus. Zacchaeus was a short and dishonest tax collector who was hated by the people that he cheated. When he heard that Jesus was coming to town, Zacchaeus climbed a tree to make sure that he could see. Jesus recognised

Zacchaeus in the tree, and told Zacchaeus that he would like to visit his house. After he had met Jesus, Zacchaeus was changed for ever.

Select one player to represent Jesus. Ask this player to stand on one side of the space, cover his or her eyes and count to thirty. Tell the remaining players that they represent Zacchaeus. While Jesus is counting, they are to hide.

When Jesus has finished counting, invite him or her to say, "Coming Zacchaeus, ready or not!" Jesus then looks for a player representing Zacchaeus. When Jesus finds one, he or she shouts, "Come out Zacchaeus, I'm staying at your house!" Everyone then comes out of their hiding places and shouts, "Hooray!" The player representing Zacchaeus then becomes Jesus, and the game may repeat.

26 Crossing The Red Sea

Bible verse: "The waters were divided, and the Israelites went through the sea on dry ground." Exodus 14:21-22.

Setting: Indoors or outdoors. A medium-sized space is required.
Number of players: Up to 20. Divide larger numbers into smaller groups.
Time: Up to 15 minutes.
Preparation: Two long ropes are required.
Age: 8-12 years.

This game is based on the story of the Israelite's escape from Egypt.

To prepare for this game, lay the long ropes on the ground, roughly two metres apart. Then, choose four players to be rope handlers. Ask the handlers to pick up the ropes and swing them like long waves. The waves may move horizontally or vertically. They may also change direction.

Ask the players to stand at one end of the ropes. The object of the game is to run between the ropes and reach the other end without being touched. One by one, invite the players to run through the ropes. If a rope touches them, they are out. If they reach the other side, they are free to try again. The last player to be untouched by a rope is the winner.

27 Samuel, Samuel!

> **Bible verse:** "Then the Lord called Samuel." 1 Samuel 3:4.

Setting: Indoors.
Number of players: Up to 30.
Time: Up to 15 minutes.
Preparation: None required.
Age: 8-12 years.

This game is based on the Bible passage in which God calls the boy
Samuel. Samuel was sleeping on a mat in Eli's house when he woke up and
heard a voice call, "Samuel! Samuel!" At first, Samuel did not know that it
was God calling him, so he went to see if it was Eli. Eli told Samuel that he
had not called him. This happened again. On the third time, Samuel
recognised that it was God and responded, "Here I am, Lord."

Ask the players to sit in a circle. Select one player to represent Samuel and
another to represent Eli. Samuel must sit in the centre of the circle,
blindfolded. To begin the game, Eli points to a player sitting in the circle.
This player calls out, "Samuel, Samuel!" in a disguised voice. Samuel must
guess who is calling his name by asking Eli, "Did (name of player) call me?"
If Samuel guesses incorrectly, Eli says, "No. Go back to sleep".

Eli then chooses another player to call out to Samuel. If Samuel guesses
correctly, Eli takes off the blindfold and places it over the eyes of the player
who called Samuel. This player then becomes Samuel, and the game
repeats.

28 David And Goliath

Bible verse: "So David and his men… left Keilah and kept moving from place to place." 1 Samuel 23:13.

Setting: Indoors or outdoors.
Number of players: Up to 20. Divide larger numbers into smaller groups.
Time: Up to 15 minutes.
Preparation: A sheet of cardboard, a cardboard box, some chalk and a small stone or ball for each player are required.
Age: 8 years and above.

This game is based on the story of David and Goliath. David, a small boy, placed his faith in God and was able to defeat the giant Goliath.

To prepare for this game, create a figure of Goliath using the sheet of cardboard. It may be realistic or symbolic. You may even wish to ask the players to make the cardboard figure as part of the game. When the figure has been created, place it on one side of the space, supported by the cardboard box. Draw a line about five metres in front of the figure, and ask all the players to stand behind it.

The aim of the game is to see who is a good enough shot to be called "David". The players must stand behind the line and attempt to knock Goliath over. If they are able to hit the figure regularly, you may wish to re-draw the line at a greater distance from the figure, and continue to do so to make the game more challenging.

29 Run, David, Run!

Bible verse: "So David triumphed over the Philistine with a sling and a stone." 1 Samuel 17:50.

Setting: Outdoors. A large space is required.
Number of players: Up to 11. Divide larger numbers into smaller groups.
Time: 10-20 minutes.
Preparation: None required.
Age: 8-12 years.

This game is based on the story of David. When David was a young man, Saul was jealous and afraid of him. Saul wanted to kill David because he was loved by God, so David fled to the wilderness to save his life. Eventually, Saul died and David was anointed king over Israel.

Prior to this game, establish a number of 'safe' areas within the space. They could be marked by trees, boxes or walls, and so on. These areas are places where David and his followers are safe from Saul.

Select one player to represent David, and invite him or her to stand on one side of the space. Divide the remaining players into two groups. The first group represents the followers of David, and must stand on the same side of the space as David. The second group represents the army of Saul, and must stand on the other side.

The aim of the game is for the followers of David to keep David safe from the army of Saul. The army of Saul must attempt to capture David by touching him or her on the shoulder. David cannot be touched when he or she is in a 'safe' area. However, David may not stay in one 'safe' area for more than 30 seconds.

Allow the game to continue for approximately five minutes. If David has not been touched within this time, ask the players to say, "Saul is dead! God has anointed David, king of Israel!" If David is touched within this time, begin the game again, and select a new player to represent David.

As Christians, we are called to live like Jesus. This call not only requires a life of faith, but also a life of example, with the attitudes and behaviour that Jesus showed. The games in this section focus on Jesus' model of Christian living and its meaning for all of us today.

30 Stamp It Out

> **Bible verse:** "If your right eye causes you to sin, gouge it out and throw it away." Matthew 5:29.

Setting: Indoors or outdoors. A large space is required.
Number of players: Any number.
Time: Up to 15 minutes.
Preparation: A permanent marker, and a balloon and 50 cm length of string for each player are required.
Age: 8-12 years.

This game is based on a passage from the Gospel of Matthew. When Jesus says, "gouge out your eye", he is not asking us to literally pluck it out. He is speaking metaphorically. Jesus means that Christians are called to give up all things that do not belong in the kingdom of God. Sometimes this is difficult, because we hold on to hurtful thoughts and ways of living. With the grace of God, all these things can be discarded.

To prepare for this game, blow up a balloon for each player and attach a length of string to its end. When this is done, talk to the players about the ways in which we can offend God and upset our friends. Ask them to discuss the ways in which we can rid our lives of these hurtful things. Then, using the permanent marker, write on each balloon something that can be stamped out of our lives. It might be a short phrase, such as "being mean", or a picture, such as a grumpy face. You may wish to ask the players to do this themselves.

Divide the players into two teams. Ask them to each tie a balloon to their ankle, using the length of string. Then, tell the players that the object of the game is for one team to stamp out all the balloons of the other. If a player's balloon is stamped out, he or she must leave the playing area. Remind the players that they are not permitted to use their hands or arms to push or shove. The winning team is the one that first manages to burst all the balloons of the other.

31 Shine Out

> **Bible verse:** "Let your light shine." Matthew 5:16.

Setting: Indoors or outdoors. A large space is required.
Number of players: A minimum of 10.
Time: Up to 15 minutes.
Preparation: A permanent marker, a balloon and a large spoon for each team are required.
Age: 8-12 years.

This game is based on Jesus' teaching about the light of the world. Jesus tells us to let our light shine, so that others may thank God.

Prior to the game, draw a flame on each of the balloons using a permanent marker. You will also need to set up a running course. Ensure that the course has a starting and finishing point (the same spot), and a marker at the opposite end for the players to run around.

Divide the players into teams of even numbers. Tell each team that they carry the light of the world, represented by the balloon. Their task is to move as quickly as they can around the marker and back, without dropping the balloon off the spoon. If the balloon is dropped, they must go back to the starting line and begin again. The light is passed from player to player, in turn. The first team to complete the course successfully is the winner.

After the game has concluded, discuss with the players the meaning of Jesus' teaching. Ask them what it means to be the 'light of the world'. Invite them to discuss the ways in which they can spread the Word of God in their own communities. Ask the players what obstacles they might encounter when doing this, and how they could deal with them. Invite them to identify the similarities between their discussion and the game.

32 Service

Bible verse: "Jesus poured water into a basin and began to wash the disciples' feet." John 13:5.

Setting: Indoors.
Number of players: A minimum of 20.
Time: 15 minutes.
Preparation: Soap, a towel and a basin filled with water are required for each group. Flour, sand, dirt, butter, margarine, oil, feathers, confetti and an odd assortment of footwear are also required.
Age: 12 years and above.

The Gospel story of the washing of the feet is a powerful illustration of Christian leadership. Jesus gives the disciples an example of how they are to lead by service.

In Jesus' day, Jesus and his disciples most likely wore sandals. This explains why many households kept a jar of water by the door, which was used to damp down people's feet before they entered the house. This task was often performed by a servant.

To begin the game, divide the players into teams of even numbers. Choose one player in each team to represent Jesus. The remaining players represent the disciples. It is not necessary to have twelve disciples for each team – four or five will be sufficient. The aim of the game is for the player representing Jesus to wash the feet of his team members as fast as possible – but the washing must be thorough.

Ask the players representing Jesus to leave the room. While they are gone, the disciples' feet must be prepared. Some may be wetted and coated in flour. Others may be covered in oil or margarine and sprinkled with confetti or feathers. Some may also be smeared with dirt or mud, while others are given shoes which are impossible to remove. Any number of ideas can be put into practice to make the washing difficult.

Now, ask the players representing Jesus to return and wash the disciples' feet. The team whose feet are washed first and most thoroughly is the winner.

After the game, discuss the meaning of the Bible passage with the players. You may wish to pose the following questions to them:

- How can we follow Jesus' example of washing the disciples' feet today?
- If Jesus' example of leadership is loving service, what does 'love' mean and require in this context?

33 Tower of Babel

> **Bible verse:** "Come, let us build ourselves a city with a tower that reaches to the heavens, so that we may make a name for ourselves." Genesis 11:4.

Setting: Indoors. A level playing surface is required.
Number of players: Any number.
Time: Up to 15 minutes.
Preparation: Several packs of playing cards are required.
Age: 12 years and above.

The story of the tower of Babel illustrates the right order of creation. In much the same way as Adam and Eve ate the fruit of the tree in order to become like God, their descendants attempted to enter God's domain by building a tower that reached to the heavens. They tried to become as powerful as God, but the building of the mighty tower soon failed.

To begin the game, divide the players into groups of four to six. Then, ask each group to build a house using the playing cards. Some groups may do very well, and construct a house that reaches high into the air. Others may not succeed at all, as their foundations continually crumble. However, all groups will find that their house of cards will eventually fall.

When the game has concluded, discuss with the players the implications of the Bible story. Ask them to identify the similarities between it and the building of the house of cards. How much of human endeavour is simply vanity, something that will soon pass?

34 Listen To The Good Shepherd

> **Bible verse:** "I am the good shepherd; I know my sheep and my sheep know me...and the sheep listen to my voice." John 10:14,16.

Setting: Indoors or outdoors. A large space is required.
Number of players: Any number.
Time: Up to 15 minutes.
Preparation: Blindfolds are required.
Age: 8 years and above.

John's Gospel contains some beautiful imagery of Jesus as the Good Shepherd. The relationship between the shepherd and his sheep is one of love and trust. The shepherd knows the sheep and the sheep know the shepherd. They listen to his voice.

This game tests the players' ability to be attentive at a purely physical level. However, many parallels can be drawn at the spiritual level. You may wish to follow this game with a discussion of the ways in which we can be attentive to God at both levels.

Ask the players to sit randomly around the room. Then, place a blindfold over each player's eyes. To begin the game, walk around the room and tap a player on the shoulder. This player must say, "I am the good shepherd." The object of the game is for the remaining players to guess who it was that spoke.

Continue the game in this fashion for a short while, before introducing some complications. For example, you may cough loudly while the player is speaking, or play some loud music. You may even instruct the player to whisper or say the phrase in a funny voice. Use these complications as a springboard to discussion of the many things that stop us from listening to the Word of God.

35 Strong Foundations

Bible verse: "Yet it did not fall, because it had its foundations on the rock." Matthew 7:25.

Setting: Indoors or outdoors. The game is best played on an uneven surface.
Number of players: 2-6. Divide larger numbers into smaller groups.
Time: Up to 30 minutes.
Preparation: A wide range of building materials, such as boxes, toilet rolls, egg cartons, plastic bottles, paper, glue and sticky tape are required.
Age: 8 years and above.

This game is based on the Parable of the Wise and Foolish Builders. In this parable, Jesus describes the foolish builder who builds his house on the sand. The house is soon swept away by the tide, as it had weak foundations. The foolish builder is contrasted with the wise builder who builds his house on the rock. This house is firm and secure, untroubled by the tide. The rock represents Jesus, the Word of God.

Ask the players to build a large house out of a range of household materials. Some of the houses may be successful, if they utilise strong foundations and careful construction. Others may not be so successful, if they are hastily built or poorly planned. The process is complicated if the surface on which they are built is very uneven. Allow the players fifteen minutes to complete this task.

At the conclusion of the game, ask the players to judge which house is the most well-built. Ask them why they chose this house over all the others. Tell the players that the best house is always the one with the best foundations. Other houses, no matter how attractive, will always be vulnerable if they have poor foundations. As part of this discussion, you may wish to test the houses that the players have built by giving them a push or picking them up. Ask the players to identify the similarities between the building of the houses and the way we live our lives. What are the foundations of our own lives? How do we know if the foundations are solid? What makes for a strong Christian life?

36 Support! Support!

Setting: Indoors or outdoors.
Number of players: A minium of 10.
Time: Up to 15 minutes.
Preparation: None required.
Age: 8 years and above.

We are all part of the Body of Christ. This means that we should strive to live together in harmony, supporting and helping one another.

In this game, the players explore the meaning of belonging to a family of faith. By working together towards a common goal, they will learn the joy of belonging to a greater body, and realise that they can only succeed if they trust one another.

Invite the players to stand in a circle, all facing in the same direction. Then, ask the players to position themselves so that the toes on their inside foot touch the inside heel of the player immediately in front of them.

Now, ask all the players to sit down, slowly and in unison. If the circle is properly formed, the rear players will support the players in front of them. However, if the circle is poorly formed, the players will not be able to support one another, and the circle will collapse. If the players cannot form a seated circle on the first attempt, ask them to continue trying until they can support one another.

If you wish, you may use this game as a springboard to discussion on what it means to be brothers and sisters in Christ, as part of the Church.

37 Get It Together

> **Bible verse:** "The body is a unit, though it is made up of many parts; and though all its parts are many, they form one body." 1 Corinthians 12:12.

Setting: Indoors or outdoors.
Number of players: Any number.
Time: 15-30 minutes.
Preparation: The construction of an obstacle course is required.
Age: 8 years and above.

This game explores the challenges of Christian living, in the context of an obstacle race. If we are to be successful as part of God's family, and not necessarily as individuals, we must respect each person's strengths and weaknesses.

The players will probably have heard that the point of participation in a game is not who wins or loses, but how the game is played. In the same way, one goal of Christian living is not to be better than anyone else, but to work together so that greater good can be achieved.

Prior to the game, you will need to design and construct an obstacle course. The course may include activities such as walking up stairs, climbing over blocks, walking up a slope or crawling through a gap. When selecting each obstacle, be mindful of the age and abilities of the players.

To begin the game, divide the players into teams of four to eight. Arrange the members of each team so that the first player faces forwards, the second player faces backwards, the third player faces forwards, the fourth player faces backwards, and so on. Then, instruct each team to complete the course as quickly and safely as they can. Tell them that they must work together to help all the members of their team.

After the game has concluded, discuss the meaning of its result with the players. If the measure of success was not who came first but how the players supported each other, were patient with each other, and cared for each other, who would have won? Why? You may wish to use this game as a springboard to discussion on the way in which the priorities of the world differ from those of Christians.

38 Parts Of The Body

Bible verse: "The body is a unit, though it is made up of many parts." 1 Corinthians 12:12.

Setting: Indoors or outdoors. A medium-sized space is required.
Number of players: Up to 20. Divide larger numbers into smaller groups.
Time: 5-10 minutes.
Preparation: Paper, sticky tape and paint are required.
Age: 3-7 years.

The message that we are all part of the body of Christ is a wonderful message for young children. It underpins the lessons they must learn to love and care for one another. This game teaches the importance of respecting each person within the body of Christ, so that together we may live in harmony and peace.

To begin this game, tell the players that St Paul describes all Christians as a body. As individuals, we are the parts of that body, which can only function properly if we all work together.

Ask the players to show you the different parts of the human body, such as the hands, feet, arms, head and back. Then, invite them to stand in a circle, with one player as the leader. Tell the leader to create an action with his or her body. For example, it might be clapping, stamping, wriggling or nodding. The remaining players watch the leader and copy the action. When everyone has joined in, move on to the next player in the circle and invite him or her to create a different action. The players then copy this action. The game may continue until all players have had a turn at being the leader.

At the end of the game, remind the children that it is important that they love and care for one another, so that the body of Christ may always work properly.

39 The Many Parts Of One

> **Bible verse:** "You are the body of Christ, and each one of you is a part of it." 1 Corinthians 12:27.

Setting: Indoors or outdoors.
Number of players: Any number.
Time: 15-30 minutes.
Preparation: Long ropes and the construction of an obstacle course are required.
Age: 8 years and above.

Like the previous game, this game explores the importance of working together to achieve a common goal. It may be used as a springboard to discussion on the model of Christian living and the meaning of belonging to Christ's Church.

Divide the players into teams of roughly equal numbers. Tie the members of each team's legs together with a long rope. Try to tie their legs in such a way that movement is extremely difficult unless they actively work together.

Now, ask the teams to attempt the obstacle course. Tell them that if one member trips or falls, then the whole team must retire. You may wish to ask the teams to attempt the course one by one, while the other teams watch. Each team will then be able to learn from the mistakes that other teams have made, and work more effectively together.

At the conclusion of the game, discuss with the players the meaning of team work. What are some similarities between team work and working together as Christians? What more is expected of Christian teams, including the Church? Why?

40 Eyes And Feet

> **Bible verse:** "The eye cannot say to the hand, 'I don't need you!' And the head cannot say to the feet, 'I don't need you!' " 1 Corinthians 12:21.

Setting: Indoors or outdoors.
Number of players: Any number.
Time: 15-30 minutes.
Preparation: Blindfolds and the construction of an obstacle course are required.
Age: 12 years and above.

This game may be used for a number of purposes. First of all, it may be used to explore the meaning of working together as Christians. Secondly, it may be used to consider the nature of trust and service. Thirdly, it may be used to nurture empathy for those who live with the disability of blindness. Lastly, it may lead into a discussion of what it means to be spiritually blind, or conversely, what it means to be a spiritual guide.

This game is played as described in the game Get It Together (Game 37), except that half of the members of each team are blindfolded. The players in each team must now work together in pairs to negotiate the obstacle course. The players without blindfolds will act as the "hands" and "eyes" of their blindfolded partners.

After the game, you may wish to discuss what the players have learned from all its aspects, or those which are the most appropriate.

41 Eyes and Feet for Juniors

> **Bible verse:** "The eye cannot say to the hand, 'I don't need you!' And the head cannot say to the feet, 'I don't need you!' " 1 Corinthians 12:21.

Setting: Indoors or outdoors, A level surface is required.
Number of players: Up to 20.
Time: 5-10 minutes.
Preparation: Blindfolds are required.
Age: 8-12 years.

Like the previous game, this game explores of the meaning of fellowship and trust. It may also be used to explore justice issues, such as caring for the disadvantaged members of our society.

To begin the game, tell the players that, as St Paul says, we all need one another. Ask them to name some people in their lives who help them and how they do so. Tell the players that when people help us over a long period of time, it demonstrates that they are trustworthy.

Now, invite the players to divide into pairs. Ask one player in each pair to volunteer to be blindfolded. Do not force anyone, as some players may find darkness very uncomfortable. Once the blindfold has been put on, ask the second player in each pair to take their partner for a walk. Instruct them to walk slowly and hold their partner by the hand. Ask them to look carefully and describe to their partner everything in their path. This way, the blindfolded player will learn to trust their partner, and gain confidence in their directions.

At the end of the game, tell the players that trust is one of the most special things that God gives us. Just as we trust people who have been kind to us over a long period of time, we can also trust God, who has loved us before we were even born.

42 Carry Each Other's Burdens

> **Bible verse:** "Carry each other's burdens." Galatians 6:2.

Setting: Indoors or outdoors. A large space is required.
Number of players: Up to 20.
Time: Up to 15 minutes.
Preparation: Sheets of paper, pens and at least forty books or other objects of a similar size are required.
Age: 12 years and above.

When Jesus commands us to love one another, he is not just speaking of sentimental love. As St Paul tells us in his letter to the Galatians, Christ's example of love includes loving service, such as carrying one another's burdens.

To begin this game, ask the players to think about the world in which they live. Invite them to name the disadvantaged groups in our world. As each group is named, compile a list that can easily be seen.

Now, ask the players to compare each of the disadvantages on the list.

If they had to measure each disadvantage by weight, how much would each weigh? To provide a basic relative unit, show them a book. Tell them that the disadvantage equivalent to the weight of one book would be experienced by those who live average lives in the Western world, with a roof over their heads, food on the table every night, education for their children and enough money to buy clothes. Ask them to compare the disadvantages of other groups in our world to this standard. Remind them that disadvantages make the load heavier.

Once all the groups on the list have been compared, tell the players that they are going to run a race. However, the race is complicated by the fact that each player must bear the weight of one of the disadvantaged groups that have just been compared. Some players may not finish the race. Some may not even be able to begin. However, instruct the players that they are able to help one another to complete the race. Together, the weight of disadvantage can be overcome, and they will be able to finish the race.

End the game by discussing with the players what it means to carry one another's burdens. You may broaden the discussion into any social justice context that you wish.

A similar game more appropriate for younger players is given below.

43 Carry Each Other's Burdens for Juniors

Bible verse: "Carry each other's burdens." Galatians 6:2.

Setting: Indoors or outdoors. A large space is required.
Number of players: Up to 20.
Time: 5-10 minutes.
Preparation: A marker pen and a cardboard box for each child are required.
Age: 3-7 years.

This game helps young players to understand that being a Christian means that we strive to help one another, just as Jesus did.

Tell the players that Jesus asks us to love one another. This means that when someone is hurt or unhappy, we should try to help them. Being hurt or unhappy is like having a heavy burden. When we help someone who is hurt or unhappy, we help to carry their burdens.

Ask the players to name some things that make them hurt or unhappy.

Ask them if they can think of any people who are hurt or unhappy. As each action or person is named, take a cardboard box and either write a word or draw a picture that illustrates the player's thoughts on it. Try to compile enough actions or people so that there is one box for each child.

Now, tell the players that the boxes represent other people's burdens. Tell them that they are going to play a game in which they carry another's burdens. They will do just what Jesus asks of them. Then, give each player a box and ask them to form a line. Invite the players to do some simple movements, such as walking, jumping or skipping with their boxes.

44 We, Who Are Strong

Bible verse: "We, who are strong, ought to bear the failings of the weak." Romans 15:1.

Setting: Indoors or outdoors. A large space is required.
Number of players: Any number.
Time: 15-20 minutes.
Preparation: Cardboard boxes of various shapes and sizes and some long feathers are required.
Age: 12 years and above.

There are many different types of strength and weakness. Some people are physically or mentally strong, while others are emotionally or spiritually strong. Similarly, some people are weak in body, but very strong in mind. Ultimately, however, all of our strength stems from God. We are supported every day by God's strength, without which we would be powerless.

To begin this game, ask the players the meaning of strength and weakness. Who are the strong and weak people in our society?

Divide the players into teams of even numbers. Tell them that they are going to have a contest to see which team is the strongest. Then, ask each team to nominate a player to hold a number of cardboard boxes, and stack the boxes in each of their arms.

While the players are holding the boxes, ask the teams to select another player to be a 'tickler'. Give each tickler a feather and tell them that they must try to make a player from a different team drop his or her boxes. However, they may only use the feather to tickle the player. Allow the 'tickers' a few minutes to attempt their task.

Once the game has concluded, discuss with the players the source of all strength in this world. How can we use this strength in our spiritual lives?

45 We Rejoice In God

> **Bible verse:** "We rejoice in the hope of the glory of God."
> Romans 5:2.

Setting: Indoors or outdoors. A large space is required.
Number of players: Up to 20. Divide larger numbers into smaller groups.
Time: 5-10 minutes.
Preparation: A large sheet, a marker pen and inflated balloons are required.
Age: 3-7 years.

Begin this game by telling the players that God loves them. God made them and gave them their families, friends and this wonderful world. God also gave them Jesus, who always helps and cares for them. Tell the players that when we think of all the things that God has given us, we feel happy.

Ask the players to name some of the wonderful things that God has given them. As they do so, take the balloons and write a word or draw a picture that represents God's great blessings. Try to put a different blessing on each balloon, and ensure that there is one for each player.

Once enough blessings have been named, place all the balloons on the large sheet. Invite the players to stand around the sheet and hold its edge. Then, ask them to hoist the sheet upwards, letting the balloons fly into the air. Invite the players to run around and catch the balloons, shouting "God has blessed me!" each time they catch one.

46 Story Mimes

Bible verse: "A happy heart makes the face cheerful."
Proverbs 15:13.

Setting: Indoors.
Number of players: Any number.
Time: 15-30 minutes
Preparation: None required.
Age: 8 years and above.

This game helps the players to explore the words and meaning of Bible passages through mime.

To begin this game, ask the players to sit in a circle. Then, select a small number of players to leave the room. Once they have left, choose a short Bible story or quotation and read it to the group. Ask the players to imagine how they would act it out.

For a selection of Bible verses, see the game Bible Quotations (Game 64).

For a selection of parables, see the game Parable Race (Game 61).

For a selection of proverbs, see the game Proverbs Charades (Game 66).

Call one of the players back into the room. Tell this player that you are going to read a short Bible story or quotation. Their task is to think of a way to mime the story to the next player.

Call the next player into the room. Tell this player that the first player will mime a Bible story or quotation. They must remember the mime so that they can repeat it to the next player. The first player then performs the mime to the second player. The first player must not use any words at all.

Call the remaining players into the room, in turn, and ask the previous player to repeat the mime to them. The final player must then guess the Bible story or quotation.

The game may be played for as long as desired, using a range of Bible stories or quotations.

47 Nursery Rhymes

> **Bible verse:** "Accept one another, then, just as Christ accepted you." Romans 15:7.

Setting: Indoors or outdoors
Number of players: Up to 12. Divide larger numbers into smaller groups.
Time: 10-30 minutes.
Preparation: Blindfolds, string and masking tape or scarves are required.
Age: 8 years and above.

This game offers players the opportunity to explore new and inclusive ways of thinking. It gives them experience in accepting and accommodating the differences of other players. This game may also be used as a springboard to discussion on the various forms of acceptance and the ways in which Jesus accepts us as we are.

To begin this game, divide the players into teams of roughly equal numbers. Ask each team to sit in a circle. Then, instruct them that three players in each team must adopt disabilities. The first player will be unable to walk, and must tie up his or her legs with string. The second player will be unable to see, and must wear a blindfold. The third player will be unable to talk, and must cover his or her mouth with masking tape or a scarf.

Tell the players that they are going to participate in a contest, in which each team must perform a well known nursery rhyme, such as "Humpty Dumpty". Instruct the players that points will be awarded for creativity (such as singing, dancing and movement), and the inclusion of all players in the performance. No player with a disability is permitted to discard their disability during the performance. The members of each team must assist one another to ensure that the performance is completed smoothly and effectively.

After the game, discuss with the players the meaning of accepting one another's weaknesses. The discussion may operate on an individual level, such as how we should deal with those who are different, or on a societal level, such as how we should treat those who are less advantaged than we are.

48 Inside Out

Setting: Indoors or outdoors.
Number of players: Up to 10. Divide larger numbers into smaller groups.
Time: Up to 15 minutes.
Preparation: None required.
Age: 8 years and above.

We are all called to be part of the body of Christ. This means that we need to love one another and work together. This game explores the meaning of being an important part of a larger body, working with others to achieve a common goal.

To begin this game, select two players and ask them to hold each other's hands. Instruct them to turn inside out, so that they are both facing outwards, but still holding hands. They must not let go of each other's hands at any stage of this exercise.

Now, ask another player to join the group. Instruct the three players to face each other and hold hands. Their task is the same: to turn inside out without letting go of one another's hands.

One by one, add more players to the group. With each new player, achieving the objective will become more complicated. Tell the players that they must work together to be successful.

At the conclusion of the game, ask the players to discuss the meaning of unity, fellowship and teamwork. Why are these things important in being part of God's Church?

49 A Gentle Word

Bible verse: "A gentle answer turns away wrath, but a harsh word stirs up anger." Proverbs 15:1.

Setting: Indoors.
Number of players: Any number.
Time: 15-30 minutes.
Preparation: Pens and sheets of paper are required.
Age: 8 years and above.

There are several passages in the Bible that deal with anger. In some circumstances anger is justified, but generally it is not. Despite this, there are many angry people in the world and in the Church. This game explores ways to deal with difficult situations and encourages the players to develop some peaceful strategies that may be put into practice.

To begin the game, divide the players into teams of roughly equal numbers. Tell each team that they must devise strategies to deal with some difficult situations. Tell them that the best strategies will attempt to diffuse each situation by using virtues such as patience, courage, respect, selflessness and compassion.

Caution the players that the best strategy will not necessarily involve giving in to another's demands, particularly if this will make them angry or upset, cause harm to another person, or require wrongful actions.

Give each team the following list of situations. You may wish to include only those situations which are appropriate for the age of the players.

1. You are reversing down the driveway and accidentally run over the next-door neighbour's cat.

2. You are at your friend's house and accidentally walk in on someone in the bathroom.

3. You are out shopping in the mall, and in a great hurry. There is a huge queue at the checkout and someone pushes in front of you.

4. Someone is constantly rude to you at school or work. He always makes you feel terrible. One day, you meet him in the park and he takes the opportunity to harass you.

5. You are out with some friends at a party. Some of your friends have been drinking and insist that they will drive home. You try to tell them that this is not a good idea, as they are probably over the legal limit. They begin to get angry, and ridicule you for being a 'chicken'.

6. You are out with some friends and notice that a girl you know has a split in the back of her dress. She is not aware of the split.

7. You are playing a team sport, and it is the grand final. One of your team members is playing very poorly. You should be winning the game, but this player continues to let the team down.

8. You are taking an important test at school. The person next to you is trying to copy your answer.

9. You are having dinner at a friend's house. Your friend's mother gives you a meal which tastes terrible. You force down a few mouthfuls, just to be polite, but they take this to mean that you want more. You do not wish to insult them by refusing, but it seems impossible for you to eat the meal without feeling sick.

10. Your sister has borrowed a special object of yours without asking. She has done this many times before, but you have asked her not to do it again. You desperately wanted to use the object, but now you must wait until she returns it.

50 On And On

> **Bible verse:** "Teaching them to obey everything I have commanded you." Matthew 28:20.

Setting: Indoors or outdoors.
Number of players: Up to 40.
Time: 10-20 minutes.
Preparation: Paper parcels are required. They can be made with sticky tape and several sheets of newspaper.
Age: 8 years and above.

Matthew's Gospel contains the great commission Jesus gives to his disciples: to build up his Church. However, Jesus does not only send the disciples on this mission – he also sends us. We play an important part in passing on the Good News of Jesus. This game explores the many different ways we can accept Jesus' commission.

Divide the players into teams of six to eight, and give each team a paper parcel. Instruct the players that they are to invent as many different ways of passing the parcel from one team member to another as possible.

Allow the teams five minutes to complete their task. Remind them that each way of passing the parcel must be unique. Once the time has passed, ask the teams to demonstrate their passing techniques to the group. The team with the most techniques is the winner.

Follow the game with a discussion of the Bible passage. You may wish to ask the players the following questions:

• What does it mean to pass on the Good News of Jesus?
• How many different ways could we pass on the Good News in our own communities?
• Why do we need to use different ways to pass on the Good News?
• How many different people could we communicate the Good News to?

A similar game more appropriate for younger players is given below.

51 On And On For Juniors

Bible verse: "Teaching them to obey everything I have commanded you." Matthew 28:20.

Setting: Indoors.
Number of players: Up to 20. Divide larger numbers into smaller groups.
Time: 5-10 minutes.
Preparation: A CD or cassette player, some Christian music, sticky tape, several sheets of newspaper and a Christian sticker, bookmark or similar gift for each child are required.
Age: 3-7 years.

The Gospel of Matthew tells us that one of Jesus' final commands to his disciples was to spread the Good News to everyone. However, it was not just up to the disciples to do as Jesus asked. We too can be involved in passing the Good News of Jesus on to others!

This game explores Jesus' command through the well known game, 'Pass the Parcel'. Just as we pass the parcel on to our friends, we can also pass the wonderful gift of Jesus' Good News on to everyone we meet.

Prior to the game, prepare the parcel by wrapping up the stickers, bookmarks or other gifts between the sheets of newspaper. Ensure that a separate piece of newspaper is placed between each gift.

To begin the game, ask the children to sit in a circle on the floor. Tell them that while the music is playing, they are to pass the parcel around the circle. When the music stops, the child holding the parcel unwraps the newspaper and receives his or her gift.

52 On And On And On!

Bible verse: "Teaching them to obey everything I have commanded you." Matthew 28:20.

Setting: Indoors.
Number of players: Up to 20. Divide larger numbers into smaller groups.
Time: 10-15 minutes.
Preparation: A CD or cassette player, some Christian music, Bibles, pens, sticky tape and several sheets of newspaper are required.
Age: 8 years and above.

This game is a further variation of On And On.

After the players have completed playing On And On (Game 50), ask them to decide on the twenty best ways to pass the parcel. Make a list of these techniques.

Ask the players to identify some of Jesus' messages that they could pass on to others. Invite them to search through the books of the New Testament and each find a short passage that describes his teachings. Then, instruct them to write down the passage on a sheet of paper, and provide a Bible reference. In order to avoid too much repetition, you may ask each team to search within a particular book, such as St Paul's letter to the Galatians, John's Gospel or the Book of Acts.

Now, invite the players to create a new parcel using the Bible quotations that they have written down. Ask them to insert the quotations between sheets of newspaper, and secure each layer with sticky tape.

The players are now ready to play 'Pass the Parcel'. Ask them to sit in a circle, and play some upbeat Christian music. Instruct the players to pass the parcel around the circle using each of the twenty passing techniques.

Stop the music occasionally, and ask the player holding the parcel to unwrap the newspaper and read out the Bible quotation.

For large groups, you may need to create several parcels. Ensure that there are no more than twenty players in each 'Pass the Parcel' game.

Some suggested Bible verses are given below:

1. "Go and make disciples of all nations."Matthew 28:19.
2. "Do not be afraid." Matthew 28:10.
3. "You are the light of the world."Matthew 5:14.
4. "Blessed are the poor in spirit."Matthew 5:3.
5. "Let the little children come to me." Matthew 19:14.
6. "Come to me all you who are weary...and I will give you rest." Matthew 11:28.
7. "Love the Lord, your God, with all your whole heart." Matthew 22:37.

53 Stand Firm

Bible verse: *"So he went down and dipped himself in the Jordan seven times."* 2 Kings 5:14.

Setting: Indoors.
Number of players: Any number.
Time: Up to 15 minutes.
Preparation: Cushions, books or other similar objects are required.
Age: 8 years and above.

In his letter to the Galatians, St Paul exhorts them to stand firm in their belief that salvation comes through faith in Jesus. The Galatians were told that faith in Jesus alone was not enough, and it was also necessary to fulfil the requirements of Mosaic law.

Like the Galatians, there are many things in our lives that can distract us from following Jesus. We must learn to stand firm in our faith, and not be led astray. This game explores the meaning of standing firm in the face of distractions and challenges.

To begin the game, divide the players into groups of six to eight players. Select one player from each group and give him or her an object such as a cushion or book. Inform these players that they are the 'balancers'. Their task is to stand firm by balancing the objects they have been given on their heads. The remaining players must try to distract the balancers so that the objects topple to the ground. Remind the players that dangerous actions such as kicking, punching or pinching are not permitted. Once an object has fallen, select a new player to become a balancer.

At the conclusion of the game, discuss with the players the meaning of 'standing firm' in a Christian context. What prevents us from standing firm as Christians? What can we do to increase our ability to stand firm?

54 It's The Limit!

Bible verse: "Humanly this is impossible but with God all things are possible." Matthew 19:26.

Setting: Indoors or outdoors. A large space is required.
Number of players: Any number.
Time: 10-15 minutes.
Preparation: A long rope is required.
Age: All ages.

This game offers players the opportunity to explore the concept of limits. What are our limits – physically, mentally and spiritually? In the Bible passage, Jesus comments on our spiritual limits. He says that there are many things that it is humanly impossible to do, but that nothing is impossible with God.

To begin this game, ask two players to hold the rope at each end. Instruct the remaining players to walk underneath the rope by bending backwards. The rope is then progressively lowered, until the players can no longer pass under it. Continue the game until no one is left.

Following the game, read Matthew 19:16-26 to the players. Then, discuss this passage with reference to the game. You may wish to ask the players the following questions:

• What limits us in our spiritual lives?
• How can we free ourselves from these limits?
• How much can we achieve on our own?

Conclude the game with silent reflection or prayer.

55 Whisper, Whisper!

Bible verse: "Everyone should be quick to listen." James 1:19.

Setting: Indoors.
Number of players: Up to 30. Divide larger numbers into smaller groups.
Time: Up to 15 minutes.
Preparation: None required.
Age: 3 years and above.

Obedience is an important quality emphasised in the Bible. It springs out of relationship and incorporates attentiveness, observation and listening. In Hebrew, the word translated as 'obedience' imparts a strong sense of listening.

In a world full of noise and busyness, many of us have lost the art of listening. We find it hard to hear God speak. This game explores the idea of shutting out all the distractions in our lives, so that we may concentrate on hearing God's voice. With older players, you may wish to use it as a springboard to discussion on the meaning of listening to God.

To begin the game, choose a Bible verse appropriate for the age of the players. A selection of verses is given below:

1. "Love one another." John 13:34. (Suitable for children aged 3-7.)

2. "A new command I give you: love one another. As I have loved you, so you must love one another." John 13:34. (Suitable for children aged 8-12.)

3. "If you love me, you will obey what I command. And I will ask the Father, and he will give you another Counsellor to be with you for ever – the Spirit of truth. " John 14:15-17. (Suitable for children aged 12 and above.)

Ask the players to sit in a circle. Whisper the Bible verse to the first player in the circle. This player must repeat the verse to the next player in the circle, and so on around the circle. Ask the last player in the circle to recite what they heard aloud.

To make the game more challenging, you may wish to introduce some distractions for the players, such as asking all those who are not whispering to whistle, shout, tap their feet, clap their hands or chat with one another. You may even play some loud music, or pretend to talk to all the players about an important matter.

At the conclusion of the game, remind the players that nothing is more important than listening to God.

58 The Sensitivity Game

> **Bible verse:** " Who touched me?" Luke 8:45.

Setting: Indoors or outdoors.
Number of players: Up to 30.
Time: Up to 15 minutes.
Preparation: A blindfold is required.
Age: 8 years and above.

Jesus was very sensitive to the people around him. He knew that a woman needed his help simply because she touched his garment. Sensitivity is an important quality to develop. When we are sensitive to someone, we can truly love and appreciate them as Jesus commanded us to. In this game, the players will discover how sensitive they are.

Ask the players to sit in a circle. Select one player to sit in the centre, blindfolded. This player's task is to identify correctly one of the players in the circle, without removing the blindfold and without moving from the centre of the circle. He or she must point to a player in the circle and say, "Who touched me?" The player in the circle then responds by saying, "I did" in a disguised voice.

Once a player is correctly identified, he or she becomes the blindfolded player and a new game begins. It is a good idea to ask the players to shift their positions in the circle at the start of each new game.

59 Blind Lead The Blind

Bible verse: "Can one blind person lead another blind person? Won't they both fall into the ditch?" Luke 6:39. (CEV)

Setting: Indoors. An area with a soft surface is required.
Number of players: Up to 10 at a time.
Time: 5-10 minutes.
Preparation: Blindfolds for each player, a long stick and a small treasure are required. It is best if the treasure makes a noise or has a distinctive smell.
Age: 8 years and above.

Jesus' question about the blind leading the blind comes within a larger passage on judgment. Jesus tells us not to judge others because we cannot see well enough to make a proper judgment. Only God has the vision to judge.

In this game, the players seek an answer to Jesus' question. You may use the game as a springboard to discussion on spiritual blindness and how this may prevent us from judging others.

Select up to ten players to form a team, and ask them stand in a line. The remaining players observe. The player at the head of the line is the leader. Give all players a blindfold, and instruct them to place it over their eyes. Then, ask the players to link hands, and give the leader the long stick.

Place the treasure somewhere in the space. When this is done, tell the players that their task is to find an object that is particularly valuable. The leader must lead them to the object safely, without any player removing his or her blindfold. Let the players proceed for up to five minutes. Once the time has passed, ask the players and observers to comment on the game. You may wish to ask them the following questions:

- How does it feel to be blind?
- How does it feel to follow someone who is blind?
- How does it feel to lead people who are blind?
- In what sense are we all blind?
- What are the consequences of our blindness when we are dealing with others?
- How does God lead us through our blindness?

60 Different Points Of View

Bible verse: "If the whole body were an eye, where would the sense of hearing be?" 1 Corinthians 12:17.

Setting: Indoors.
Number of players: Any number.
Time: Up to 15 minutes.
Preparation: A photocopy or overhead transparency of the template is required.
Age: 12 years and above.

In this Bible passage, St Paul speaks about spiritual gifts and the meaning of belonging to God's Church. He describes how each of us brings unique gifts to Christian living, and how these individual differences create a rich diversity. This game offers the players an opportunity to explore this concept in a concrete way. As each player explains what he or she sees in the transparency, the remaining players have the opportunity to experience the transparency from a different point of view. This helps them to understand that we all see things slightly differently, and that each person's perspective can be valid and valuable.

To begin the game, show the players the template. Ask them to study it for a moment and name the objects that they can see. Most likely, the players will have various opinions about which is the most prominent object.

Once the players have expressed their opinions, discuss with them the ways in which we are all different. Ask them how these differences add value to our lives together. Invite the players to consider their own gifts and the various ways in which they can contribute to the life of the Church.

TEMPLATE 1:

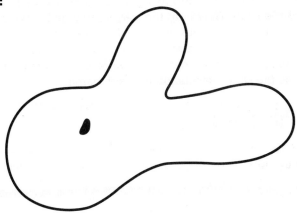

Note 1. You may need to enlarge this image or copy it on to an overhead transparency.

Note 2. Do you see the duck, the rabbit, the fish, the letter Y, the saddle or some other images?

The duck image faces the right and the two lobes form the duck's beak. The rabbit faces left and the two right lobes are the rabbit's ears. The fish also faces the left and the lobes form the tail of the fish. The entire image is shaped like a saddle. (Author note: I had never seen the saddle until I played this game with children who lived in rural areas. A saddle was the first image that they saw.)

These types of images can be found in numerous psychology text books.

The games in this section are designed to increase the players' familiarity with the Bible itself. They help the players to gain knowledge of the books and stories of the Bible, and develop skills necessary to find Bible passages. The games are also ideal to be played indoors on cold or rainy days. As Bible translations can vary considerably, it is best to ensure that all players use the same translation for each game.

61 Parable Race

> **Bible verse:** "I speak to them in parables." Matthew 13:13.

Setting: Indoors.
Number of players: Any number.
Time: 15-30 minutes.
Preparation: Pens, sheets of paper, Bibles and copies of the Bible references listed below are required.
Age: 8 years and above.

This game allows the players to improve their skills in using the Bible. In order to play the game, they must be able to identify the various books of the Bible and find various references within these books. The game is helpful for those who are just beginning to be familiar with the Bible, and also for those who already have some knowledge of its layout.

The aim of this game is for each team to write down the titles of a number of parables from their Bible references. They must search for each parable in the Bible, and write down its title as listed. Some parables and their references are given below. Select a number and variety of parables suitable to the ages of the players. For example, four to five parables from the same Gospel would be suitable for players aged 8-12, while four to eight parables from different Gospels would be suitable for players aged 12 years and above.

To begin the game, divide the players into teams of equal numbers. Give each team a list of Bible references, a Bible, a sheet of paper and a pen. On the word, "Go!", instruct the teams to search through their Bibles for the parable's name, and write it down on their sheet. The first team to correctly list the names of all parables is the winner.

1. Parable of the Sower.
    Matthew 13:3-9, also Luke 8:5-8

2. Parable of the Weeds (also called the Parable of the Darnel).
    Matthew 13:24-30

3. Parable of the Mustard Seed.
    Matthew 13:31-32, also Luke 13:18-19

4. Parable of the Yeast.
    Matthew 13:33, also Luke 13:20-21

5. Parable of the Treasure.
    Matthew 13:44

6. Parable of the Pearl of Great Price.
    Matthew 13:45-46

7. Parable of the Lost Sheep.
    Matthew 18:10-14, also Luke 15:3-7

8. Parable of the Lamp.
    Luke 8: 16-18

9. Parable of the Good Samaritan.
    Luke 10:30-35

10. Parable of the Lost Coin (also called the Parable of the Lost Drachma.)
    Luke 15:8-10

11. Parable of the Prodigal Son (also called the Parable of the Lost Son).
    Luke 15:11-32

12. Parable of the Crafty Steward (also called the Parable of the Shrewd Manager).
    Luke 16:1-8

13. Parable of the Rich Man and Lazarus.
    Luke 16:19-31

14. Parable of the Persistent Widow.
    Luke 18:2-8

15. Parable of the Pharisee and the Tax Collector.
    Luke 18:10-14

16. Parable of the Pounds (also called the Parable of the Ten Minas).
    Luke 19:12-27, also Matthew 25:14-30

17. Parable of the Wicked Tenants.
    Luke 20:9-16, also Matthew 21:33-41

18. Parable of the Workers in the Vineyard.
    Matthew 20:1-16

19. Parable of the Wedding Banquet.
    Matthew 22:1-14

20. Parable of the Ten Virgins.
    Matthew 25:1-13

62 Advanced Parable Race

Bible verse: "But to others, I speak in parables." Luke 8:10.

Setting: Indoors.
Number of players: Any number.
Time: 15-30 minutes.
Preparation: Pens, sheets of paper, Bibles and a copy of the Bible references listed in Game 61 are required.
Age: 8 years and above.

This game is played as described above in Parable Race, except that each team must also write down a short summary of each of the parables assigned to them. The first team to compile a list of all the parables and their summaries is the winner.

For players aged 8-12, it is sufficient for each team to write a one or two sentence outline of each parable's plot. For older players, you may prefer to ask for a longer summary of the meaning of each parable.

63 Matthew, Mark, Luke And John

Bible verse: "People live...on every word that comes from the mouth of God." Matthew 4:4.

Setting: Indoors.
Number of players: Any number.
Time: Up to 15 minutes.
Preparation: Pens, sheets of paper, Bibles and a copy of the list of Bible stories given below are required.
Age: 8 years and above.

This game encourages the players to familiarise themselves with Gospel stories.

Some of the stories about Jesus appear in all four Gospels, while others appear in two or three Gospels. The stories listed below are written in only one Gospel.

Divide the players into teams of roughly equal numbers. Give each team a Bible, a sheet of paper, a pen, and a copy of the list below. Ask them to write down the name of the Gospel in which each story appears. The winning team is the first one to correctly identify the correct Gospel for each story. For younger players, you may wish only to use some of the stories listed below.

1. The three Magi visit the baby Jesus.
    (Matthew.)

2. The angel Gabriel tells Mary that she will bear a child named Jesus.
    (Luke.)

3. Jesus washes the disciples' feet.
    (John.)

4. Thomas doubts that Jesus has risen.
    (John.)

5. The Parable of the Prodigal Son.
    (Luke.)

6. Zacchaeus meets Jesus.
    (Luke.)

7. The boy Jesus is lost in the Temple.
    (Luke.)

8. The woman caught in adultery is brought to Jesus.
    (John.)

9. The Parable of the Good Samaritan.
    (Luke.)

10. Jesus meets two disciples on the road to Emmaus.
    (Luke.)

11. Mary and Joseph flee with baby Jesus to Egypt.
    (Matthew.)

12. The good thief is crucified beside Jesus.
    (Luke.)

13. Jesus asks John to look after his mother Mary.
    (John.)

14. The Parable of the Rich Man and Lazarus.
    (Luke.)

15. Jesus commands his followers to spread the Good News.
    (Matthew.)

64 Bible Quotations

> **Bible verse:** "Their children, who do not know this law, must hear it."
> Deuteronomy 31:13.

Setting: Indoors.
Number of players: Any number.
Time: 30-60 minutes.
Preparation: Sheets of paper, pens and Bibles are required.
Age: 8 years and above.

This game gives the players familiarity with quotations from the Bible. Divide the players into teams, and ensure that each team is provided with a Bible, sheets of paper and pens. Then, tell the players that you will read to them a number of incomplete quotations from the Bible. Their task is to complete the quotations.

Begin by reading the first incomplete quotation, along with a few additional words that the players will need to find. Allow each team two minutes to check their answer, using a Bible. After the time is up, proceed to the next quotation. Again, give the players some key words from the second part of the quotation, and allow them two minutes to check their answer. Continue in the same manner for all the quotations given below.

To assist in completing the quotations, you may wish to give younger players the Bible reference for each quotation, or the book from which it comes. The team that completes the most quotations correctly is the winner.

The following quotations are taken from the New International Version. As different Bible translations can vary considerably, it is best to ensure that all players use the same translation, and the wording for the first part of each quotation is taken from that translation.

1. "In the beginning was the Word, and...
    ...the Word was with God, and the Word was God."
    John 1:1-2

2. "And Mary said,'My soul glorifies the Lord, and...
    ...my spirit rejoices in God, my saviour.' "
    Luke 1:46-47

3. "Blessed are you who are poor,...
...for yours is the kingdom of God."
Luke 6:20-21

4. "Do not judge and you will not be judged. Do not condemn and you will not be condemned...
...Forgive and you will be forgiven."
Luke 6:37-38

5. "You are the light of the world...
...A city on a hill cannot be hidden."
Matthew 5:14-15

6. "Jesus declared,'I am the bread of life.Whoever...
...comes to me will never go hungry.' "
John 6:35

7. "But I tell you: love your enemies and...
...pray for those who persecute you."
Matthew 5:44-45

8. "I am the true vine, and my Father...
...is the gardener."
John 15:1-2

9. "As the Father has loved me, so...
...have I loved you."
John 15:9

10. "But store up for yourselves treasure in heaven, where moth and rust do not destroy and...
...where thieves do not break in or steal."
Matthew 6:20-21

11. "Greater love has no one than this, that...
...he lay down his life for his friends."
John 15:13-14

12. "Ask and it will be given to you; seek and you will find;...
...knock and the door will be opened to you."
Matthew 7:7

13. "My Lord and...
...my God."
John 20:28

14. "But small is the gate and narrow the road that leads to life, and...
...only a few find it."
Matthew 7:14-15

15. "Come to me, all you who are weary and burdened, and...
    ...I will give you rest."
    Matthew 11:28

16. "And I tell you, it is easier for a camel to go through the eye of a needle than...
    ...for the rich to enter the kingdom of God."
    Matthew 19:24-25

17. "I am the Good Shepherd. The Good Shepherd...
    ...lays down his life for the sheep."
    John 10:11-12

18. "I am the Good Shepherd; I know my sheep and...
    ... my sheep know me."
    John 10:14

19. "Consider how the lilies grow. They do not labour or spin. Yet, I tell you...
    ...not even Solomon in all his splendour was dressed like one of these."
    Luke 12:27

20. "I am the resurrection and the life. He who believe in me...
    ...will live, even though he dies."
    John 11:25

65 Parable Charades

Bible verse: "But to others, I speak in parables." Luke 8:10.

Setting: Indoors.
Number of players: Up to 12.
Time: 15-30 minutes.
Preparation: None required.
Age: 8 years and above.

This game tests the players' knowledge of Jesus' parables.

To begin this game, divide the players into teams of equal numbers. Then, select one player in each team to act as a 'mimer'. The mimer's task is to convey a parable to the other players without using sounds or words.

The mimer may choose to act out either the name or the story of the parable. The other players must guess the name of the parable. Once the parable has been correctly guessed, allow a new mimer to convey a different parable. The game continues until all players within the team have had a turn at miming.

For a list of parables, see Parable Race (Game 61).

66 Proverbs Charades

Bible verse: "The wise in heart are called discerning."
Proverbs 16:21.

Setting: Indoors.
Number of players: Up to 10. Divide larger numbers into smaller groups.
Time: 15-30 minutes.
Preparation: Envelopes containing a number of proverbs (see below) on separate pieces of paper are required.
Age: 8 years and above.

This game tests the players' knowledge of proverbs from the Bible.

To begin the game, divide the players into groups of roughly equal numbers. Give each group an envelope. Then, select one player from each group to act as a 'mimer'. Invite the mimer to choose one proverb from the envelope. Instruct the mimer not to look at the other proverbs, as they will be used later.

The mimer's task is to convey the proverb to the group without using sounds or words. The other players must attempt to guess the proverb. If the players have difficulty in guessing a proverb, suggest that the mimer takes one word of the proverb at a time. The mimer lets the players know when they have guessed this word correctly. The player that correctly guesses the proverb becomes the next mimer.

Some suggested proverbs are given below:

1. "Pride goes before destruction." Proverbs 16:18.
2. "Pleasant words are a honeycomb." Proverbs 16:24.
3. "The way of the sluggard is blocked with thorns." Proverbs 15:19.

4. "Children with good sense make their parents happy." Proverbs 15:20.(CEV)

5. "A happy heart makes the face cheerful" Proverbs 15:13.

6. "A generous person will prosper." Proverbs 11:25.

7. "Where there are no oxen, the manger is empty." Proverbs 14:4.

8. "The fear of the Lord is a fountain of life." Proverbs 14:27.

9. "A whip for the horse, a halter for the donkey and a rod for the backs of fools." Proverbs 26:3.

67 Knowledge Of The Secrets

Bible verse: "The knowledge of the secrets of the kingdom of heaven has been given to you." Matthew 13:11.

Setting: Indoors.
Number of players: Any number.
Time: Up to 15 minutes.
Preparation: Bibles, pens and paper are required.
Age: 8 years and above.

This is a decoding game that may be played individually or in teams. It increases the players' knowledge of the Bible, and gives them familiarity with Jesus' teachings.

Ask the players to find one of Jesus' well-known sayings from the Bible, such as "I leave you peace". Then, ask them to develop a code. Some suggestions are listed below:

1. Put all the letters of the saying together. For example, "I leave you peace" becomes, "ileaveyoupeace". Then, divide the saying into short words, such as "ile avey oup ea ce".

2. Select a number to correspond with each letter in the alphabet. For example, the letter "a" could be 1, the letter "b" could be 2, the letter "c" could be 3, and so on. The saying "I leave you peace" then becomes: 9, 12, 5, 1, 22, 5, 24, 15, 21, 16, 5, 1, 3, 5.

3. Replace each letter in the saying with the letter immediately before it in the alphabet. For example, the saying "I leave you peace" becomes "h kdzud xnt odzbd".

4. Replace each letter in the saying with the letter immediately after it in the alphabet. For example, the saying "I leave you peace" becomes "j mfbwf zpv qfbdf".

Once the code is complete, ask the players to pass the encoded message to another player or team for decoding. The winner is the first player or team to decode the message correctly.

68 Love, Joy, Peace, Patience

> *Bible verse:* "The fruit of the spirit is love, joy, peace, patience, kindness, goodness, faithfulness, gentleness and self control."
> Galatians 5: 22-23.

Setting: Indoors or outdoors. A space with a large wall and a level floor is required.
Number of players: Up to 4. Divide larger numbers into groups of 4.
Time: 15-30 minutes.
Preparation: A bouncing ball is required for each group.
Age: 8 years and above.

This is a ball game which helps players memorise the fruits of the Spirit, as described in St Paul's letter to the Galatians.

The aim of the game is for each player to complete the sequence described below, without dropping or fumbling the ball. If the ball is dropped, the turn is passed to the next player.

When all the players have had their first turn, the first player resumes where he or she last left off. The game continues until all players have successfully completed the entire sequence.

The sequence is as follows:

1. Love: Throw the ball at the wall and catch it on the rebound. Do this nine times. Each time, say the word "love".

2. Joy: Throw the ball at the wall, allow it to bounce once, and then catch it. Do this eight times. Each time, say the word "joy".

3. Peace: Using alternate hands, bounce the ball on the ground seven times. Catch it after the seventh bounce. On each bounce, say the word "peace".

4. Patience: Lifting your left or right leg, throw the ball at the wall and

catch it on the rebound. Do this six times. Each time, say the word "patience".

5. Kindness: Throw the ball at the wall, clap your hands once and catch it on the rebound. Do this five times. Each time, say the word "kindness".

6. Goodness: Throw the ball at the wall, clap your hands twice and catch it on the rebound. Do this four times. Each time, say the word "goodness".

7. Faithfulness: Throw the ball at the wall, spin your body around once and catch it on the rebound. Do this three times. Each time, say the word "faithfulness".

8. Gentleness: Throw the ball at the wall, touch the ground with both hands and catch it on the rebound. Do this twice. Each time, say the word "gentleness".

9. Self control: Throw the ball in the air, spin your body around once and catch it on the rebound. Say the word "self control".

10. Bounce the ball nine times and on each bounce say one of the gifts of the Holy Spirit, so that by the end of the bounces each of the gifts has been said.

69 Recollections

Bible verse: "I wrote about all that Jesus began to do and teach." Acts 1:1.

Setting: Indoors.
Number of players: Up to 10. Divide larger numbers into smaller groups.
Time: Up to 15 minutes.
Preparation: None required.
Age: 8 years and above.

This is a memory game which increases the players' familiarity with people, places and events from the Gospels.

To begin the game, ask the players to sit in a circle. Invite the first player in the circle to name a person, place or story from Jesus' life. For example, they might mention John the Baptist, Bethlehem or Christmas. The next child in the circle must then repeat this person, place or story and add another, such as Zacchaeus, Jerusalem or Easter.

The game then continues around the circle, with each player trying to remember all the words that have already been said and adding one more. Players must leave the game if they can't remember the words that have already been said or can't add another word. The winner is the last person playing.

70 The Wisdom Of Solomon

Bible verse: "Give your servant a discerning heart." 1 Kings 3:9.

Setting: Indoors.
Number of players: Any number.
Time: Up to 15 minutes.
Preparation: Photocopies of the riddle activity sheets and pens are required.
Age: 10 years and above.

This game is a fun way for players to test their general Bible knowledge. It may be played by individuals or teams.

Ask the players to solve the following riddles. The first player or team to complete the riddles has the Wisdom of Solomon!

Who am I?

I am a spot, a speck, a stain. I am also a book of the Bible. My name has four letters. The first is in "mystery". In the last three, Noah sailed the oceans.

I am Mark.

What am I?

I am a place mentioned in the Bible. Water is normally green or blue, but in my case, it is a different colour.

I am the Red Sea.

What am I?

My first is a vegetable, small, green and round.
My second looks just like a snake on the ground.
My last four are very good things to do;

You give them to those who have less than you.
All my six, sing all day and all night;
Songs of praise, songs of power,
Thanksgiving and delight.
I'm a book of the old, not of the new.
King David had something to do with me, too.

I am the book of Psalms.

71 The Beatitudes

Bible verse: "Blessed are the poor in spirit..." Matthew 5:3.

Setting: Outdoors. A level playing surface is required.
Number of players: Up to 6. Divide larger numbers into groups of 6.
Time: 15-30 minutes.
Preparation: Chalk and a small stone for each player are required.
Age: 8 years and above.

The Beatitudes provide the outline of Jesus' example of Christian living. This game increases the players' familiarity with the Beatitudes, and encourages them to follow this example in their daily lives.

This game is based on hopscotch. To prepare for the game, draw a hopscotch template on the ground using the chalk. You will need to draw nine squares large enough to write one of the Beatitudes in each square. When the template is complete, write "Blessed are..." on the ground before the first square. The Beatitudes may then be added by writing one of the following phrases in each square:

1. The poor in spirit.
2. Those who mourn.
3. The meek.
4. The righteous.
5. The merciful.
6. The pure in heart.
7. The peacemakers.
8. Those persecuted for justice's sake.
9. Those who keep faith.

To begin the game, ask the players to form a line and give each player a stone. Invite the first player to throw his or her stone at the first square. If it lands in the square, the player must say, "Blessed are the poor in spirit". The player then bends down and picks up the stone, without putting a foot in the first square, and hops in every other square. After the last square, the player exits the game and allows the next player a turn.

Players who fail to throw their stone in the correct square, put their second foot down, step in the square with the stone, fail to hop in all the appropriate squares or fail to say the Beatitude must go to the back of the line and try again. Players who fail three times in a row must leave the game.

Once the first round of the game is completed, the players proceed to throw their stones at the second square ("Blessed are those who mourn"). If successful, they may move on to the third square, then the fourth square, and so on until the ninth square.

TEMPLATE 2

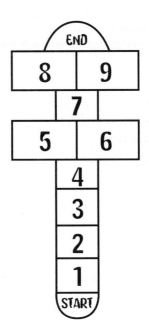

Note: For game 72, utilise the 'End' space as square number 10.

72. The Ten Words

> **Bible verse:** "And God spoke all these words." Exodus 20:1.

Setting: Outdoors. A level playing surface is required.
Number of players: Up to 6. Divide larger numbers into groups of 6.
Time: 15-30 minutes.
Preparation: Chalk and a small stone for each player are required.
Age: 3 years and above.

The Ten Words (also called the Ten Commandments) that Yahweh gave to Israel are the basis for right living. This game helps the players to remember the Ten Commandments in an enjoyable way.

To prepare for the game, draw a hopscotch template on the ground using the chalk. (See diagram.) You will need to add a tenth square at the end of the grid for this game. You will need to draw ten squares large enough to write one of the Ten Commandments in each square. They may be written as follows:

1.   Put God first.
2.   Worship only God.
3.   Keep God's name holy.
4.   Keep the Sabbath for God.
5.   Honour your family.
6.   Don't kill.
7.   Be faithful in marriage.
8.   Don't steal.
9.   Don't lie.
10.   Don't covet others' things.

The game may then be played as described above for The Beatitudes. For younger players you may need to say the words in each square and the children can jump from square to square rather than hop from square to square.

73 Bible Skips

Bible verse: "Impress (my words) on your children."
Deuteronomy 6:7.

Setting: Indoors or outdoors. A medium-sized space is required.
Number of players: Up to 10. Divide larger numbers into smaller groups.
Time: 10-20 minutes.
Preparation: A long skipping rope and a number of Bibles are required.
Age: 8 years and above.

One of the continuing themes in the Book of Deuteronomy is the need to pass on the word of God. This includes passing on the organisation of the Bible. In this game, the players become familiar with all the books of the Bible, and learn their order from Genesis to Revelation.

Before beginning the game, ask the players to look at the Table of Contents in the Bible. Together, read through the names of each book in the Bible, so that players can familiarise themselves with the pronunciation. This may need to be repeated once or twice.

To begin the game, ask two players to turn the skipping rope. Instruct the remaining players to form a line in front of the rope. Then, one by one, invite them to jump into the skipping rope.

The object of the game is for the players to complete as many skips as possible without stepping or tripping on the rope. As each player skips, the remaining players recite or read the books of the Bible in order, starting with Genesis and continuing until Revelation.

This list is used as a measure of how many skips have been completed. To make the game more challenging for older players, you may wish to ask the players to recite the books in reverse order.

If a player misses a skip, he or she must move aside and let the next player take a turn. The game may continue for as long as desired, or until all players know the books of the Bible.

74 Genealogy

Bible verse: "A record of the genealogy of Jesus Christ."
Matthew 1:1.

Setting: Outdoors.
Number of players: Up to 10. Divide larger numbers into smaller groups.
Time: Up to 15 minutes.
Preparation: A long skipping rope and a number of Bibles are required.
Age: 8 years and above.

This game is played as described above for Bible Skips, except that Jesus' genealogy is used as a measure of how many skips have been completed.

It helps the players to remember the genealogy of Jesus.

Before beginning the game, it is recommended that you read through Jesus' genealogy with the players, so that they can practice the pronunciation of each name. This may need to be repeated once or twice.

Again, the object of the game is for the players to complete as many skips as possible without stepping or tripping on the rope. As each player skips, the remaining players say Jesus' genealogy in order, from Abraham to Jesus:

Abraham, Isaac, Jacob, Judah,

Perez, Hezron, Ram, Amminadab,

Nahshon, Salmon, Boaz, Obed,

Jesse, David, Solomon, Rehoboam,

Abijah, Asa, Jehosaphat, Jehoram,

Uzziah, Jotham, Ahaz, Hezekiah,

Manasseh, Amon, Josiah,

Jeconiah, Shealtiel, Zerubbabel, Abiud,

Eliakim, Azor, Zadok, Akim,

Eliud, Eleazar, Matthan, Jacob, Joseph,

Husband of Mary,

Mother of Jesus.

75 The Twelve Apostles

Bible verse: "These are the names of the twelve apostles: first, Simon..." Matthew 10:2.

Setting: Indoors or outdoors. A level playing surface is required.
Number of players: 4-8. Divide larger numbers into smaller groups.
Time: Up to 15 minutes.
Preparation: A strip of elastic at least 6 millimetres (.23 inch) wide and 4 metres (4.37 yards) long is required.
Age: 8 years and above.

This game assists young players to remember the names of the twelve apostles.

To prepare for the game, tie the strip of elastic together at the ends. Then, invite two players to stand inside the elastic, with their legs slightly apart. This forms an elastic rectangle.

The object of the game is for the players to perform one of the following sequence of jumps, while saying the name of an apostle. If a player fails to execute a jump or fails to say the correct name of an apostle, they must take the place of one of the elastic holders, who then joins the jumping queue.

The jumping sequence is as follows:

1. Simon-Peter: jump to the left-hand side of the elastic rectangle.
2. Andrew: jump to the right-hand side of the rectangle.
3. James: jump into the middle of the rectangle.
4. John: jump so that each foot lands on an elastic, one foot on the left and one foot on the right.
5. Philip: jump and turn around so that each foot lands on an elastic, facing the opposite direction.
6. Bartholomew: jump into the middle of the rectangle.
7. Thomas: jump to the left-hand side of the rectangle.
8. Matthew: jump into the middle of the rectangle.
9. James: jump so that each foot lands on an elastic, one foot on the left and one foot on the right.

10. Thaddaeus: jump and turn around so that each foot lands on an elastic, facing the opposite direction.

11. Simon: jump so that each foot lands outside the elastic.

12. Judas: jump out of the rectangle to the left or right.

Begin the game with the elastic strip at ankle height. As the game progresses, the elastic may be raised as high as you wish.

Section 4 Games Based On Parables, Proverbs And Images

The games in this section focus on Jesus' parables, the proverbs of the Old Testament and the imagery used in the Bible. They enable the players to explore biblical concepts through many different means, such as physical activity, storytelling and improvisation. The last game of this section also provides the players with an opportunity to deconstruct a parable, in order to explore its meaning and message in depth.

76 The Mustard Seed

> **Bible verse:** "The kingdom of God is like...a mustard seed which is the smallest seed you plant in the ground. Yet, when planted, it grows and becomes the largest of all garden plants, with such big branches that the birds of the air can perch in its shade." Mark 4:30-32.

Setting: Indoors or outdoors.
Number of players: Any number.
Time: 5-10 minutes.
Preparation: None required.
Age: 3-7 years.

This game introduces the players to to the Parable of the Mustard Seed.

Begin by dividing the players into two groups. One group represents the mustard seeds, and the other represents the birds of the air. Invite the first group to walk into the centre of the space and crouch down on the floor like tiny little mustard seeds. The birds of the air then sit in a circle around the mustard seeds and say:

"The mus-tard seed,

the mus-tard seed,

the mustard seed is the smallest seed."

After the rhyme has been said, the mustard seeds pretend to grow and grow until they are big trees with spreading branches. As this is happening, the birds of the air say:

"It grows and grows and grows, you see,

until it is a mustard tree."

Once the mustard trees are fully grown, the birds of the air jump up and pretend to fly towards them, saying:

"And all the birds, they all agree:

the best place is the mustard tree."

When they have reached the mustard trees, the birds of the air must sit down. The game may then be repeated as often as desired.

77 The Narrow Gate

Bible verse: "Enter through the narrow gate." Matthew 7:13.

Setting: Indoors or outdoors. A large space is required.
Number of players: Up to 30.
Time: Up to 15 minutes
Preparation: None required.
Age: 8 years and above.

This game is based on Jesus' teaching of the narrow gate. In this teaching, Jesus contrasts the broad gate that leads to destruction with the narrow gate that leads to life. It is very easy to walk through the broad gate, but very hard to walk through the narrow gate.

Start by telling the players the parable. Select two players to represent the gate. Ask them to stand facing each other, some distance apart and with their arms outstretched. Instruct the remaining players to stand back from the gate.

The object of the game is for the players to run through the gate without being caught. The players representing the gate begin the game by saying the following rhyme:

"We are the gate! We are the gate!

Enter through the narrow gate!"

As soon as the rhyme has been said, the players rush through the gate. Each gate must attempt to catch another player. The players that are caught then become the gate. If no players are caught, the same players continue as the gate for the next game.

To emphasize the difference between the wide and narrow gates, play the game several times. Start with the players representing the gate standing far apart, so that many players are able to pass through. Then, in the following games, ask them to stand progressively closer together, so that fewer and fewer players are able to pass through.

78 Wise Builders, Foolish Builders

> **Bible verse:** "A wise man built his house on the rock."
> Matthew 7:24. See also Luke 6: 49.

Setting: Indoors or outdoors.
Number of players: Up to 20. Divide larger numbers into smaller groups.
Time: 5-10 minutes.
Preparation: None required.
Age: 3-7 years.

This game is based on Jesus' teaching of the two house builders. In this teaching, Jesus says that anyone who hears his words and puts them into practice is like a wise man who builds his house on the rock. The rain may come and the wind may blow, but the house still stands. Jesus also says that anyone who ignores his words is like a foolish person who builds his or her house on the sand. When the rain and wind come, the house falls down.

To begin the game, ask the players to form a circle and hold hands. Instruct them to sing the following rhyme, to the tune of "Ring-A-Ring O' Roses". Accompany the rhyme with the actions indicated below:

(Skip around the circle.)

"Build your house upon the sand,

Build it near the shore."

(Fall down.)

"Oh no, oh no!

It all falls down!"

(Walk around the circle in a crouched position.)

"Build your house upon the rock:

It will be quite firm."

(Jump up.)

"Oh yes, oh yes!

We all stand up!"

79 Knock, Knock! Let Me In!

Bible verse: "Knock and the door will be opened to you."
Matthew 7:7. See also Luke 11:9.

Setting: Indoors or outdoors. A large space is required.
Number of players: Up to 30.
Time: 5-10 minutes.
Preparation: None required.
Age: 3-7 years.

This game is based on Jesus' teaching about prayer. Jesus says that if we knock at the door and ask, God will be there waiting to let us in. This means that we must pray to God, because God loves us and wishes to give us many good things.

To begin the game, tell the players the parable. Then, select a player to represent the doorkeeper. Instruct this player to face a wall and cover his or her eyes. Direct the remaining players to stand on the opposite side of the space.

Now, ask the players to repeatedly whisper, "Knock, knock! Let me in!" as they walk towards the doorkeeper. Instruct them to speak a little louder each time they repeat the phrase. At some point, the doorkeeper must call out "Yes, yes! I'll let you in!" The players then run to the doorkeeper and shout, "Thank you, doorkeeper. You have let us in!"

The game may be repeated as often as desired. Select a different player to represent the doorkeeper each time.

80 Bright Light

Bible verse: "You are the light of the world." Matthew 5:14.

Setting: Indoors or outdoors.
Number of players: Any number.
Time: 5-10 minutes.
Preparation: None required.
Age: 3-7 years.

This game is based on Jesus' teaching about the light of the world. In this teaching, Jesus tells us that we are a bright light that should shine forth for others to see.

To begin the game, ask the players to form a circle. Then, say the following rhyme with them, accompanying it with the actions indicated below:

(Wiggle your fingers like a flickering flame.)

"Twinkle, twinkle, little light,

Shining, shining, shining bright."

(Trace the outline of a sphere with your fingers, to represent the world.)

"Shine for all the world to see,

Shine for you and shine for me."

(Shake your index finger to indicate "no".)

"Do not let that light go out,

Do not put that bright light out."

(Wiggle your fingers like a flickering flame.)

"Twinkle, twinkle, little light,

Shining, shining, shining bright."

81 Hidden Treasure

Bible verse: "The kingdom of heaven is like treasure hidden in a field." Matthew 13:44.

Setting: Indoors or outdoors. A space with many hiding places is required.

Number of players: Any number. Divide larger numbers into teams of 8-10.

Time: 30-60 minutes.

Preparation: One sheet of white cardboard, cut into seven strips, and a Bible, pen and sheet of paper for each team are required.

Age: 12 years and above.

This game is based on the Parable of the Treasure in the Field, in which Jesus compares the kingdom of God to a hidden treasure. Just like the man who sold everything he had to inherit the buried treasure, we must search for the treasure of God's kingdom and hold it close to our hearts when we have found it.

Prior to the game, write the references of seven Bible verses on the strips of white cardboard. For a selection of Bible verses, see the game On And On And On (Game 52). Once this is completed, hide the strips in the playing area. Try to find as many ingenious hiding places as possible. Finally, stack the Bibles in the centre of the space.

Instruct the players that they are going to participate in a treasure hunt. Tell them that that they will need to listen carefully to the instructions, as there are two steps that they must complete in order to win.

Tell the players that seven treasures have been hidden in the playing area. Each treasure contains a Bible reference. The first task for each team is to find all seven treasures and write down their Bible references. The second task is for them to use a Bible to find each of the seven references. The teams must copy the Bible verses on to their sheets of paper. The first team to complete both tasks correctly is the winner.

In fairness to all players, teams are not permitted to move a treasure once they have found it. However, they may try to mislead other teams by pretending that a treasure is in a place that it is not.

As an extension of this game, you may wish to ask the players to memorise the Bible verses. The first group which correctly recites all ten verses is the winner.

82 The Lost Sheep

Bible verse: "Suppose one of you has a hundred sheep and loses one of them. Does he not leave the ninety nine in the open country and go after the lost sheep until he finds it?" Luke 15:4.

Setting: Indoors or outdoors. A large space is required.
Number of players: A large number.
Time: Up to 15 minutes.
Preparation: A whistle, a small object to represent a sheep for each team and the construction of an obstacle course are required (see below).
Age: 8-12 years.

In Luke's Gospel, there are three parables of the lost: the Parable of the Lost Sheep, the Parable of the Lost Coin and the Parable of the Lost Son. In each parable, the main character searches for something that is lost and rejoices when it is found. This is just like God's relationship with us.

This game is based on the Parable of the Lost Sheep. In this parable, when the shepherd finds that one of his sheep is lost, he leaves his flock and searches in the wilderness – a very dangerous place in Jesus' time – until the sheep is found. God is just like this shepherd. God seeks us out when we stray and always welcomes us home.

Prior to the game, you will need to design an obstacle course. Ensure that the course contains:

• An object to crawl under or through;

• An object to circle seven times;

• An object to climb over.

You will also need to find or prepare some small objects to represent the lost sheep. They could be fluffy toys, pillows or toilet rolls covered with cotton wool. Ensure that there is one lost sheep for each team, and place them at the end of the obstacle course.

To begin the game, divide the players into teams of even numbers. Ask the teams to line up at the start of the obstacle course. Then, tell the players that the object of the game is for each player to run through the obstacle course, pick up a lost sheep and return to the start of the course. When a lost sheep has been retrieved, the next player in the team starts the obstacle course, while the previous player returns the lost sheep to the end.

If any player drops a lost sheep, they must return to the start of the obstacle course and begin again. The first team to complete the course successfully is the winner.

A similar game more appropriate for younger players is given below.

83 The Lost Sheep for Juniors

> **Bible verse:** "Your Father in heaven is not willing that any of these little ones should be lost." Matthew 18:14.

Setting: Indoors or outdoors.
Number of players: Any number.
Time: 5-10 minutes.
Preparation: None required.
Age: 3 years and above.

Like the previous game, this game is based on the Parable of the Lost Sheep.

To begin the game, select one player to represent the Good Shepherd. Tell the remaining players that they represent the lost sheep. The Good Shepherd must stand facing a wall and cover his or her eyes.

Ask the Good Shepherd to count to twenty while the lost sheep hide. Once the Good Shepherd has finished counting, instruct him or her to say: "I am the Good Shepherd". The Good Shepherd then looks for the lost sheep until they are all found. The last sheep to be found replaces the Good Shepherd and a new game may begin.

84 The Lost Coin

> **Bible verse:** "Search carefully until (you) find it." Luke 15:8.

Setting: Indoors or outdoors.
Number of players: Any number.
Time: 15-30 minutes.
Preparation: A sheet of silver cardboard, blank paper and pens are required.
Age: 8 years and above.

This game is based on the Parable of the Lost Coin. In this parable, a woman loses a coin and searches her house very carefully until she finds it. When she discovers the coin, she calls her friends and neighbours together to rejoice. Jesus tells us that just as the woman rejoices over the finding of the lost coin, so heaven rejoices when God finds us.

To prepare for this game, cut ten circles out of the sheet of silver cardboard, each roughly the size of a jam jar lid. They represent the lost coins. Write a short Bible verse on each one. A selection of verses is set out in Bible Quotations (Game 64).

Once the coins have been created, hide them in various places. Then, gather the players together and tell them that you have lost ten special coins. It is their task to locate all ten coins. When they find a coin, instruct the players to write down its Bible verse on a sheet of paper. To make the game fair for all, tell them that the coins must not be removed from their original hiding places.

A similar game more appropriate for younger players is given below.

85 The Lost Coin for Juniors

Bible verse: "Rejoice with me. I have found my lost coin!"
Luke 15:9.

Setting: Indoors or outdoors.
Number of players: Up to 30.
Time: Up to 15 minutes.
Preparation: A number of circular objects, such as bottle tops, jar lids and buttons, and aluminium foil are required.
Age: 3-7 years.

Like the previous game, this game is based on the Parable of the Lost Coin.

To prepare for the game, wrap the circular objects in shiny paper or aluminium foil, to make them look like coins. Then, hide them in various places.

Once the objects have been hidden, tell the players that you have lost some special coins. Instruct them to find the coins, and shout out, "I have found a coin! " when they have done so.

86 One Taken, One Left

> **Bible verse:** "Two men will be in the field: one will be taken and the other left." Matthew 24:40.

Setting: Indoors or outdoors. A level playing surface is required.
Number of players: Up to 8. Divide larger numbers into smaller groups.
Time: 10 minutes.
Preparation: Chalk, one marble for each player and two distinctive marbles are required.
Age: 8 years and above.

In Matthew's Gospel, Jesus tells his disciples to be prepared, as they do not know when he will return. This game may be used as a springboard to discussion on how we can prepare ourselves for the coming of Jesus.

To prepare for the game, draw two circles on the ground with the chalk. Make the first circle approximately two metres in diameter, and draw the second inside this circle. Then, place the two distinctive marbles inside the small circle.

Explain to the players that one of the distinctive marbles represents the man who was taken, while the other represents the man who was left behind. One by one, invite them to try to shoot one of the distinctive marbles out of the small circle. Tell them that they must do this without touching the other distinctive marble, and without putting their hands inside the large circle.

87 Sheep And Goats

> **Bible verse:** "And he will separate the people one from another as a shepherd separates the sheep from the goats." Matthew 25:32.

Setting: Indoors.
Number of players: Up to 10. Divide larger numbers into smaller groups.
Time: 15-30 minutes.
Preparation: A handful of light wooden skewers and roll of coloured tape are required.
Age: 8 years and above.

This game is based on the teaching of the sheep and goats, in which Jesus speaks about the time when we will all be judged. At the final judgment, God will separate those who followed Jesus from those who did not. This game explores Jesus' imagery in a concrete way.

To prepare for the game, cut off the tips of the skewers using scissors or secateurs. Then, stick a small strip of coloured tape on half of the skewers. The coloured skewers represent the sheep, and the other skewers represent the goats.

To begin the game, drop the skewers to the ground so that they fall in a heap. Tell the players that their task is to pick the sheep and goats out of the heap and place them in two separate piles. However, no skewer may be moved in the process of picking up another. One by one, invite the players to remove a skewer from the pile. Any player who moves or drops a skewer misses a turn. The game continues until all the sheep are separated from the goats.

Following the game, discuss the meaning of the Bible passage as follows.

- Jesus invites us to love one another as he loved us. Sometimes making loving choices can put us at odds with other people. Have you ever experienced this?
- What can help us to make loving choices?

88 The Judge Said "No!"

> **Bible verse:** "A widow... who kept coming to him with the plea, 'Grant me justice.' " Luke 18:3.

Setting: Indoors.
Number of players: 4-6. Divide larger numbers into groups of 4-6.
Time: Up to 15 minutes.
Preparation: Pens and sheets of paper are required.
Age: 8 years and above.

This game is based on the Parable of the Persistent Widow. Jesus tells the story of a wronged widow who annoys a judge until he gives in to her demands.

The parable operates on a number of levels. At one level, it is a story about God's justice. In Jesus' time, a woman without a man to represent her had no standing in Jewish society. She would have been ignored by judges, and at the mercy of all others. If her plea was not answered, she would have been reduced to begging or prostitution. At this level, Jesus tells us that God hears the voices of the most helpless and invisible members of society. At another level, it is also a story about the power of prayer. If we persist in our prayers to God, all our needs will be met.

To begin this game, read the following poem to the players:

The widow went to the judge's door.

"Give me justice," the widow said.

"No!" said the judge as he slammed the door

And took himself back to bed.

The widow knocked on the judge's door.

"Give me justice!" she cried through the lock.

"No!" said the judge, as he stopped up the hole

With glue and a great big rock.

The widow climbed on the judge's roof.

"Give me justice!" she called down the flue.

"No!" cried the judge up the chimney pipe

And went to hide in the loo.

The widow stood in the judge's yard

And shouted with all her might.

"Go!" said the judge, "and don't come back

Or you'll have a great big fight!"

The widow started a street parade.

"Give her justice!" the marchers cried.

High in the air, the judge threw his hands.

"I'll give her justice!" he sighed.

Invite the players to think about all the funny things that the widow might do to get the judge's attention. Then, ask each group to write either a humorous poem or story about the widow and the judge. When the poems and stories are complete, you may wish to read them to all the players.

Following the game, discuss with the players the meaning of justice. You may wish to pose the following questions:

• Who are the 'widows' in our own society?

• How can we answer their pleas?

• What is God's justice?

• How can we use prayer to assist the course of God's justice?

89 Sheep and Thieves

Bible verse: "I am the gate for the sheep." John 10:7.

Setting: Indoors or outdoors. A large space is required.
Number of players: Up to 25. Divide larger numbers into smaller groups.
Time: Up to 15 minutes.
Preparation: None required.
Age: 8 years and above.

This game is based on the Parable of the Sheep's Pen. In this parable, Jesus compares himself to the gate through which the sheep must pass to enter the safety of the pen.

To begin this game, ask the players to stand in a circle. Tell them that the circle represents the sheep's pen. Then, select two to four players to represent the sheep, and two players to represent the thieves. The sheep should stand inside the circle, and the thieves outside the circle.

The aim of the game is for the thieves to break through the sheep's pen and touch the sheep. The sheep, however, must avoid being touched. The players in the circle may assist the sheep by blocking the thieves with their arms. Once a sheep has been touched, the game begins again. Select new players to represent the sheep and thieves.

With older players, you may use this game as a springboard to discuss the ways in which Jesus cares for us. Some questions you may wish to pose are:

*   Who are the sheep in our own day and age? What qualities do they have?

*   Who are the thieves? What qualities do they have?

*   How do we ensure that we stay inside the pen and not outside with the thieves?

90. The Vine And The Branches

> **Bible verse:** "I am the vine, you are the branches." John 15:5.

Setting: Indoors.
Number of players: Up to 12. Divide larger numbers into smaller groups.
Time: Up to 15 minutes.
Preparation: None required.
Age: 12 years and above.

This game is based on Jesus' imagery of the vine and the branches. Jesus compares himself to a vine and his people to its branches. Just as the branches rely upon the vine for support and sustenance, so all of Jesus' followers draw strength and sustenance from him. We should try to follow his example of Christian living, but at the same time use our individual gifts and talents for the greater glory of God. This game explores these concepts through the use of rhythm and beat.

To begin the game, ask the players to sit or stand in a circle. Then, select one player to represent the vine. Invite this player to start a basic beat using a part of the body. For example, the beat may be tapped, clapped, stamped or sung.

When the beat has been established, instruct the player representing the vine to nod to the player on his or her right. This player represents one of the branches, and must add a rhythm that follows the beat. When the rhythm is established, this player nods to the next player in the circle. This player adds a new rhythm which complements the first. However, the two rhythms should not be the same. When both rhythms are synchronised with the beat, the third player nods to the next player in the circle, and a fourth player establishes another rhythm. The game continues until all players are in accord.

Following the game, discuss with the players the meaning of being a follower of Jesus. You may wish to ask them the following questions:

- How is it that we are all different and yet still one in Jesus ?

- What challenges do individual differences present to the followers of Jesus?

- What opportunities do these differences present?

91 The Yeast And The Leaven

> **Bible verse:** "The kingdom of heaven is like yeast...mixed into a large amount of flour, until it worked all through the dough." Matthew 13:33.

Setting: Indoors.
Number of players: Any number.
Time: Up to 15 minutes.
Preparation: A CD or cassette player and some upbeat Christian music are required.
Age: All ages.

This game is based on the Parable of the Yeast. In this parable, Jesus compares the kingdom of God to the small amount of yeast that a woman kneads into a large amount of dough. The small amount of yeast leavens the entire batch of dough. In the same way, Jesus tells us that the kingdom of God is spread by sharing the life and love of Jesus with everyone we meet.

To begin the game, ask the players to sit in a circle. Play some upbeat Christian music and select one player to begin a basic dance. Tell the players that the dancer is like the yeast. He or she has begun a dance that will eventually spread through the whole group.

Instruct the dancer to continue dancing around the group, and occasionally tap another player on the shoulder. When a player is tapped, he or she must join the dance by forming a line behind the head dancer. The game then continues until all the players are dancing.

At the conclusion of the game, discuss with the players the meaning of the kingdom of God. You may wish to pose the following questions:

- What does Jesus mean when he compares the kingdom of God to the small amount of yeast?
- How can we help Jesus to make this kingdom grow?

92 The Net

Bible verse: "The kingdom of heaven is like a net that was let down into the lake and caught all kinds of fish." Matthew 13:47.

Setting: Indoors or outdoors. A level playing surface is required.
Number of players: Up to 4. Divide larger numbers into smaller groups.
Time: 5-10 minutes.
Preparation: A small flat stone for each player, ten additional small flat stones and a small amount of paint are required.
Age: 8 years and above.

This game is based on the Parable of the Net. In this parable, Jesus tells us that the kingdom of God is like a net that was lowered into a lake and collects many fish. Some fish are caught and others are not.

To prepare for the game, place a small daub of paint on five of the ten additional stones. Once the paint has dried, drop all the ten stones on the ground. Tell the players that the painted stones represent the fish that are to be caught, while the other stones represent the fish that are not caught. Their task is to pick up the fish that are caught without moving any of the other fish. To do this, they must throw their stones in the air and attempt to scoop up one or more of the caught fish before their stone hits the ground.

Players who move any of the fish or fail to catch their stone in time must pass their turn to the next player. The game continues until all the caught fish are caught.

Following the game, discuss the parable with the players. You may wish to ask them to reflect on the following:

- Have you ever experienced a time when you were left out of a group? How did you feel? Why do you think you were left out?

- Think about a group of people such as children in your class, people in your church, groups in your town, city or country. Why are some people considered to be 'in' or 'out' of a group?

- Jesus tells us that everyone is welcome in the kingdom of God. What would the world be like if everyone was 'in' and no one was left 'out'?

93 Twenty Excuses

> **Bible verse:** "But they all alike began to make excuses." Luke 14:18.

Setting: Indoors.
Number of players: Any number.
Time: 15-30 minutes.
Preparation: Sheets of paper and pens are required.
Age: 8 years and above.

This game is based on the Parable of the Great Banquet. In this parable, the invited guests all had excuses as to why they could not attend the feast. Similarly, we often make excuses in our daily lives as to why we cannot do as Jesus asks.

To begin this game, divide the players into teams of equal numbers. Give each team a sheet of paper and a pen, and allow them fifteen minutes to invent twenty excuses as to why the guests could not attend the great banquet. The excuses may be ridiculous, such as "my cat had a hair ball", or serious, such as "there was a flash flood".

Once the excuses have been invented, ask each team to share them with the group. Invite the players to vote on the best excuse. Conclude the game by discussing with the players the excuses that prevent them from committing their lives completely to Jesus.

94 Who Is Part of God's Kingdom?

> **Bible verse:** "So the servants went into the streets and gathered all the people they could find, both good and bad, and the wedding hall was filled with guests." Matthew 22:10.

Setting: Indoors or outdoors.
Number of players: Any number.
Time: 5-20 minutes.
Preparation: A long skipping rope is required.
Age: All ages.

This game is based on the Parable of the Wedding Feast. In this parable, a king prepares a great wedding feast for his son, but many of the invited guests refuse to come. So the king asks his servants to gather all the people they can find in the streets, and bring them to the wedding hall.

In one sense, this parable refers to Jesus' reception by the Jews and his further ministry to the Gentiles. In another, it tells us that we are all part of God's kingdom.

To begin the game, select two players to turn the skipping rope. Instruct the remaining players to line up in front of it. Then, ask the following question about the first player in the line: "Is (name of player) part of God's kingdom?" Invite everyone to respond: "Yes! (Name of player) is part of God's kingdom!" Once the response has been said, ask the first player to jump through the skipping rope. Continue the game in the same fashion for all players in the line, and also ensure that the rope handlers are included.

If the game is played with family groups, you may wish to ask the questions in a more general way, such as, "Are dads part of God's kingdom?", or "Are sisters part of God's kingdom?", or "Are babies part of God's kingdom?", and so on. After each of question, invite all the people named to jump through the rope. In the case of babies or elderly people, it may be best to stop the rope and let them walk across.

A similar game more appropriate for younger players is given below.

95 Who Is Part Of God's Kingdom? Variation

Bible verse: "So the servants went out into the streets and gathered all the people they could find, both good and bad, and the wedding hall was filled with guests." Matthew 22:10.

Setting: Indoors or outdoors.
Number of players: Any number.
Time: 5-20 minutes.
Preparation: A hula hoop or a large ring.
Age: All ages.

This is a variation of the previous game. In this game, the players will learn that we are all part of God's kingdom.

Begin the game by telling the players that God loves them and has a special place for them in his kingdom. Then, ask the players to form a line. Stand at the head of the line with the hula hoop or large ring. Then, ask the following question about the first player in the line: "Is (name of player) part of God's kingdom?" Invite everyone to respond: "Yes! (Name of player) is part of God's kingdom!" Once the response has been said, ask the first player to jump through the hoop. Continue the game in the same fashion for all players in the line.

96 Parable Board Games

Bible verse: "The secret of the kingdom of God has been given to you. But to those on the outside, everything is said in parables." Mark 4:11.

Setting: Indoors.
Number of players: Any number.
Time: 1-3 hours.
Preparation: Bibles, sheets of paper, pens, scissors, glue, sticky tape, colouring and drawing materials, a number of small jar lids or other circular objects, dice for each group, large sheets of coloured cardboard (enough for each group to have at least one sheet each), and large sheets of white cardboard (enough for each group to have one and a half sheets each) are required.
Age: 10 years and above.

Part of the purpose of a parable is for us to place ourselves in the picture that it paints. This allows us to use our imagination to explore its meaning. In this game, the players will make their own board games to explore the meaning of a parable.

This is a long game with several steps. It is best to divide the players into groups of six or less, and ask them to do the steps in order, as follows:

Step 1
Choose one parable from the following list:
1. Parable of the Lost Coin. Luke 15:8-10
2. Parable of the Lost Sheep. Luke 15:4-6
3. Parable of the Persistent Widow. Luke 18:2-5
4. Parable of the Mustard Seed. Luke 13:18-19

Read the parable and break it down into its story elements. For example, if

you have selected the Parable of the Persistent Widow, the story elements
might be:

1.   A widow has been wronged.
2.   She goes to the house of a judge, looking for justice.
3.   The judge ignores the widow's demands.
4.   The widow persists.
5.   The judge gives her justice.

Step 2

Elaborate on each story element within the parable. For example, in the
case of the Parable of the Persistent Widow, you might ask the following
questions:

1.   What did the widow do to persist?
      - Did she knock on the windows?
      - Did she knock on the door? Did she climb on the roof?
      - Did she march up and down the judge's front yard, chanting
        slogans?
2.   What did the judge do in response to the widow's persistence?
      - Did he board up the house?
      - Did he call for the guard?
      - Did he try to leave the house by the back door?
3.   What happened when the judge finally gave in?

Invite the players to write their ideas down on a sheet of paper.

Step 3

Imagine the elaborated story as a board game.

In the case of the Parable of the Persistent Widow, the starting point of the
game would be the widow being wronged, and the end point would be the
judge giving her justice. Between these two points, a number of events
could have occurred. Some of the spaces on the board game will contain
these possible outcomes. Other spaces will contain an instruction, such as
"move back two spaces", "miss a go", "roll again" or "move forward one
space." Some spaces will also be left blank.

Now, look at your elaborated story to identify a number of the possible outcomes. What events would warrant the widow missing a go? For example, it could be the judge boarding up the house. What events would warrant rolling the dice again? For example, it could be the widow catching the judge at the back door. Once you have identified these outcomes, make a plan for the board game on a sheet of paper.

Step 4

Create the board game.

Using the jar lids or other circular objects, cut out sufficient circles from the sheet of white cardboard for each space in the board game. Number each circle, and write on them the instructions for each space. For example, an instruction could be, "Widow climbs on the roof. Move forward one space." Remember to leave a small number of spaces blank. Cut out two additional circles for the start and the finish of the game. You may wish to decorate these spaces with illustrations or designs.

Arrange the spaces on the sheet of coloured cardboard. They may be linked in any shape you wish. Some possible designs are a spiralling circle or a snaking line. Glue the spaces in their places, according to your plan.

Step 5

Create characters for the players to use as they play the game.

Cut out four circles from the sheet of white cardboard and draw a character on each. Make sure that each character is distinguishable from the others. In the case of the Parable of the Persistent Widow, you might create a number of widows, each in a different coloured dress.

Step 6

Gather your group together, and begin playing your board game!

Prayer is an integral part of Christian living. The games in this section provide fun ways to introduce people of all ages to prayer.

97 One, Two, Three, Four

> *Bible verse:* "I always thank God." 1 Corinthians 1:4.

Setting: Indoors or outdoors.
Number of players: 2-12. Divide larger numbers into smaller groups.
Time: Up to 15 minutes.
Preparation: None required.
Age: 6 years and above.

It is always good to remember the many gifts that God has given us. This game helps the players to celebrate God's abundant love through a prayer of thanksgiving.

Invite the players to sit in a circle, with their hands held out in front of them. Then, select one player to be the leader. The leader begins the game by saying the following rhyme:

"One, two, three, four,

We thank God for ever more!

Thank you, God, for…"

On the first beat of the rhyme, the leader gently taps the left hand of the player to the right of them in the circle. This player then taps the left hand of the player to the right of them, and so on around the circle, to the beat of the rhyme.

The player who is tapped on the last beat of the rhyme must select something for which to thank God. This player then becomes the leader, and the game repeats.

With older players, you may wish to ask the player who is tapped on the last beat of the rhyme to spell something for which to thank God. For each letter, this player must tap the left hand of the players around the circle. The player who is tapped on the last letter then becomes the next leader.

98 Five, Six, Seven, Eight

> **Bible verse:** "They should always pray and not give up." Luke 18:1.

Setting: Indoors or outdoors.
Number of players: 2-12. Divide larger numbers into smaller groups.
Time: Up to 15 minutes.
Preparation: None required.
Age: 6 years and above.

In thanksgiving, we turn our hearts to God in gratitude. In praise and worship, however, we stand in awe of God's power and might. This game is played in the same way as One, Two, Three, Four, (Game 97) except that it is based on a prayer of praise, rather than a prayer of thanksgiving.

The leader begins the game by saying the following rhyme:

"Five, six, seven, eight,

Our God is great!

We praise you God for…"

The game then continues as described above. As a variation, the players may wish to tap one another's feet instead of their hands.

99 Spin The Bottle

> **Bible verse:** "Is anyone of you in trouble? You should pray. Is anyone happy? Sing songs of praise." James 5:13.

Setting: Indoors or outdoors.
Number of players: 2-12. Divide larger numbers into smaller groups.
Time: Up to 15 minutes.
Preparation: An empty plastic bottle is required.
Age: 6 years and above.

This game is based on a prayer of thanksgiving. It gives the players an opportunity to praise and thank God for his mighty and wonderful works.

Ask the players to sit in a circle, with the empty bottle in the centre. Invite one player to spin the bottle. The player to whom the bottle points begins the game by saying the following prayer:

"God is good, God is great!

All the world did God create!

God made land and God made seas,

Animals, insects, flowers and trees!

Thank you, God, for all of these,

Especially..."

This player must then name something for which he or she wants to thank God. Once the intention has been said, the player spins the bottle, and the game begins again. Tell the players that they are free to say an original prayer in place of the prayer written above.

This longer game is designed to help older players explore the nature of justice. It is best played with twenty or more players, and should be played over an extended period of time, up to six hours. This allows the players to discuss a number of concepts related to justice in depth, and without the pressure of short time constraints.

100 The Justice Game

> **Bible verse:** "He… will settle disputes for strong nations far and wide." Micah 4:3.

Setting: Indoors.
Number of players: Up to 60.
Time: 3-6 hours.
Preparation: Photocopies of the activity sheets for each team, pens, string, scarves or headbands, and blindfolds are required.
Age: 12 years and above.

General Overview

This is a game about leadership and social justice.

Divide the players into at least three teams. Each team forms a country. Some countries are rich and have few problems, while others are poor and have many problems.

During the game, the countries compete against one another in a series of contests. As the game proceeds, the economic conditions of the various countries will change. Generally, the rich countries become richer, but they may plunge into economic difficulty due to ineffective leadership. Similarly, the poor countries generally become poorer, but they may reverse their economic situation through effective government.

At regular intervals, the countries meet together at the United Nations (U.N.) forum. During this forum, each country is required to address its economic and social problems, as well as those of the world. This is achieved largely through debate, but may also be achieved through monetary means. Each country may use the U.N. forum to buy and sell resources (convert asset tokens into cash), grant and ask for loans, establish and dissolve alliances, demand payment, forgive debts, or even declare war. Countries may also spend money to solve social problems.

Discussions in the U.N. may become heated as countries disagree on the best course of action. However, the U.N. has a guiding charter to which each country must adhere. This charter contains six fundamental principles, sourced from the Bible. The principles are intended to ensure that the interests of each country are balanced against the interests of the world and conform to God's plan.

Preparation

Before beginning the game, ensure that you have available:

- At least one adult to act as a convenor of the U.N. (see below);
- Sufficient photocopies of the "Country Profile" and "Comprehension Challenge" activity sheets for each team;
- Money tokens and asset tokens for each country, placed in envelopes clearly marked with the name of each country;
- A large photocopy of the guiding principles of the U.N.;
- A number of extra money tokens to be given to the winner of each contest;
- Headbands or scarves for players who cannot talk;
- A ball of string for players who cannot walk;
- Sufficient blindfolds for players who cannot see;
- Marker cones to construct a running track for a relay race; and
- A baton for each team.

How To Play The Game

Step 1

Ask each team to choose a letter from either U, N or S. The letter U stands for United Commercial States (U.C.S.), the letter N stands for New Findersland, and the letter S stands for Simbalia.

Assign each team to their respective country, and provide them with the relevant "Country Profile" activity sheet (see below). Ask them to complete the details on the sheet. If more than one team chooses the same letter, simply add a number after the name of the country to distinguish them, such as "Simbalia 1" and "Simbalia 2".

To begin, countries should not know the financial situation of other countries.

Step 2

Ask the members of each team to select a president, a treasurer, two U.N. representatives, and their disabled people, as directed by the activity sheet. Invite each team to create a motto for their country.

Step 3

Instruct each team to prepare their disabled people. String should be used to tie the legs of those who cannot walk, headbands or scarves to bind the mouths of those who cannot speak, and blindfolds to cover the eyes of those who cannot see. The disabled players must remain disabled for the entire game, unless they are cured. It costs $100 to cure a disability, and any money spent in this way must be given to the U.N. treasury.

Step 4

Provide the treasurers of each country with the envelopes containing their money and asset tokens.

Step 5

The countries are now ready to compete against each other in a series of contests. It costs $50 to participate in a contest The winning country receives $100.

The contests are as follows:

1. Each team must produce an original performance of a well known religious song. If the group is not overly familiar with religious songs, choose a nursery rhyme instead. Marks will be awarded for creativity, involvement of all players, and the use of song and dance. Marks will be deducted for players who do not participate. Allow each team 15-30 minutes to prepare their performance. The team with the highest marks is the winner.

2. Each team must complete the maths challenge, which is provided on the activity sheet. The first team to provide correct answers to all the questions is the winner. Please note that the answers have been set out on the bottom of the sheet. These should not be included when the sheets are given to the participants.

3. Each team must participate in a relay race. All players must compete, and each disabled player may be assisted by one helper from the same team. The first team to cross the finish line is the winner.

4. Each team must memorise the following Bible passage:
   "A new command I give you: love one another. As I have loved you, so

you must love one another. By this all will know that you are my disciples." John 13:34-35. The first team able to recite the passage aloud is the winner.

Step 6

Between each contest, instruct the members of each team to withdraw from the game and discuss the state of their country. For example, they may discuss their financial situation, the number of people with disabilities, or the course of action necessary to ensure that they remain competitive in the contests.

Step 7

Between each contest, invite each country to convene at the U.N. forum and discuss the present state of the world. Each country which sits in the U.N. is required to pay a fee of $50. The U.N. representatives from each country form a small circle in the centre of the room, while the other players sit in a larger circle around the outside. The U.N. representatives are then given the opportunity to speak on behalf of their country. They may wish to express their grievances, make demands or requests, spend some money to cure their disabled people, or form an alliance with another country. Only the U.N. representatives are permitted to speak during the forum, although they may ask to consult the members of their country briefly.

Step 8

Draw the U.N. forum to a close, and invite the countries to compete in the next test. Follow this again with discussion and a U.N. forum.

Convenors of the United Nations

One or more adults are required to act as convenors of the United Nations. The convenors have the following tasks:

1. Collect $100 from countries which decide to cure a disability;
2. Announce the format and beginning of each contest;
3. Supervise each contest and adjudicate the performances of the religious song or nursery rhyme;
4. Award $100 to the winner of each contest;
5. Collect $50 from each country which attends a U.N. forum and collect $50 from each country that participates in a contest;
6. Call the U.N. into session;

7. Act as chairperson of the U.N. and draw attention to its five guiding principles when necessary; and

8. Decide when to draw the game to a conclusion.

As a complication to the game, the convenors may randomly introduce a variety of "wild cards". Wild cards are unexpected events which have widespread implications on the world situation. Their purpose is to make each country think about the uncertainty of the future and how they can respond to unexpected circumstances.

A wild card may be an event similar to the following:

- A flash flood devastates Simbalia. Simbalia loses $50 and gains two more people with disabilities. The U.C.S. and New Findersland must also pay $50 to the UN to help with relief work.

- A new technology is developed. Only countries with more than $200 in their treasury may take advantage of the technology, for which they earn $100.

- A new industrial initiative requires a country with cheap labour costs. Only countries with under $100 in their treasury may decide to support the initiative, for which they receive $100.

The Conclusion

The game may conclude at any time. The aim of the game is not to run poor countries into such huge financial debt that they are no longer able to survive. Nor is it for the rich countries to expand their economies so much that they lose interest in the state of the world around them. The purpose of the game is to enable players to experience "injustice" and its consequences and to see how productive debate within the U.N. can be, as countries struggle to balance their own interests against the interests of the whole world.

Following the conclusion of the game, you may wish to ask the players to reflect on their experiences. Discussion can be wide ranging depending on the maturity of the players and can include the following:

- How does wealth and poverty affect a country, affect countries in dealing with each other and affect the world?

- How difficult is it to see something from another's point of view. What are the consequences of this at an individual and societal level?

- What is the relevance of Christianity in the world today?

- What does justice mean?

- What does divine justice require?

County Profile 1

U.C.S. (United Commercial States)

You are the biggest and most industrialised country in the United Nations. You have a strong treasury, with $400 in reserve. You also have $400 worth of assets. Only one person in U.C.S. has a disability.

Your president is _____.

Your treasurer is _____.

Your representatives on the U.N. are _____

and _____.

Your disabled person is _____.
This person is unable to see.

Tokens

$50	$50
$50	$50
$50 assets	$50 assets
$50 assets	$50 assets

Reproduce as needed.

Country Profile 2

New Findersland

Your country is small but industrialised in a number of areas. You have a reasonably strong economy, with $200 in the treasury and $200 worth of assets. Two people in New Findersland have disabilities.

Your president is _____.

Your treasurer is _____.

Your representatives on the U.N. are _____

and _____.

Your disabled people are _____

and _____.
One person is unable to see, and the other is unable to walk.

Tokens

$50	**$50**
$50	**$50**
$50 assets	**$50 assets**
$50 assets	**$50 assets**

Reproduce as needed.

Country Profile 3

Simbalia

Your country is very large but under-developed in many areas. You are a poor third world country, with a struggling economy. Your treasury has $100, and you have $100 worth of assets. You have five disabled people.

Your president is _____.

Your treasurer is _____.

Your representatives on the U.N. are _____

and _____.

Your disabled people are _____,

_____, _____,

_____ and _____.

One person is unable to see, two people are unable to walk, and two people are unable to speak.

Tokens

$50	$50
$50 assets	$50 assets

Reproduce as needed.

114

Guiding Principles
of
The United Nations

1. "Do not judge and you will not be judged. Do not condemn and
   you will not be condemned. Forgive and you will be forgiven...
   A good measure pressed down... will be poured into your lap.
   For with the measure you use, it will be measured to you."
   Luke 6:37-38.

2. "A new command I give you: love one another. As I have loved
   you, so you must love one another." John 13:34-35.

3. "Jesus called them together and said, 'You know that the rulers of
   the Gentiles lord it over them, and their high officials exercise
   authority over them. Not so with you. Instead, whoever wants to
   become great among you must be your servant, and whoever
   wants to be first must be your slave.' " Matthew 20:24-27.

4. " The king will reply, 'I tell you the truth, whatever you did for
   one of the least of these brothers (and sisters) of mine, you did
   for me.' " Matthew 25:37-40.

5. "And what does the Lord require of you? To act justly and to love
   mercy and to walk humbly with your God." Micah 6:8.

Additional money tokens for the U.N.

$50	$50	$50
$50	$50	$50
$50	$50	$50
$50	$50	$50
$50	$50	$50
$50	$50	$50
$50	$50	$50

Maths Challenge Activity Sheet

The Bible includes a number of descriptions which include numerical quantities in ancient units of measure.

The recipe for the Oil of Chrism is given in Exodus 30:22-24. It lists the quantities of liquid myrrh, fragrant cinnamon, fragrant cane and fragrant cassia required in units called shekels. Roughly speaking, one shekel is equivalent to ten grams.

Similarly, there were a number of stone jars at the wedding in Cana (John 2:1-12) , each holding 30 gallons. A gallon is equivalent to 4.5 litres.

Your task is to:

1. Find the number of shekels of liquid myrrh, fragrant cinnamon, fragrant cane and fragrant cassia listed in the recipie for the Oil Of Chrism;

2. Convert the measures of each ingredient in the Oil of Chrism into grams;

3. Find the number of stone jars present at the wedding in Cana;

4. Combine the volumes of all the jars present at the wedding in Cana and convert this value into litres.

The first team to complete the task successfully is the winner.

Answers

1. 500 shekels liquid myrrh, 250 shekels fragrant cinnamon, 250 shekels fragrant cane, 500 shekels fragrant cassia.

2. 5000 grams liquid myrrh, 2500 grams fragrant cinnamon, 2500 grams fragrant cane, 5000 grams cassia.

3. 6 stone jars.

4. 810 litres.

Bibliography

Abba, K. and Abrahams, J. Jesus Rap. (Sydney: Circadian Rhythms, 2000).

Abba, K., Abrahams, J. and O'Brien, M. Great Times With Jesus. (Sydney:Willow Connection, 2003).

Adams, S. The Great Games Book. (London: Dorling Kindersley, 1997).

Allen, E.B. 100 Bible Games. (Michigan: Baker Book House, 1996).

Anderson, D. Encyclopaedia of Games. (Michigan: Zondervan, 1954).

Barry, S.A. Giant Book of Puzzles and Games. (New York: Sterling Publishing Co., 1997).

Bompiani, E. E. Games for all Seasons. (London: Carousel Books, 1976).

Eisenberg, H. and L. Fun with Skits, Stunts and Stories. (Michigan: Baker Book House, 1975).

Howard,V. Fun Games for Boys and Girls. (Michigan: Zondervan, 1974).

Keeler, R.F. Bible Games and Activities. (Michigan: Baker Book House, 1982).

Magee, L. 201 Group Games. (Michigan: Baker Book House, 1983).

McKenzie, J. and Bledsoe, S. The Big Book of Bible Games and Puzzles. (Michigan: Zondervan, 1971).

Silver, L.Great Kids' Games. (Bowral: Sally Milner Publishing, 1999).

Wakerman, M. and Graham, L.S. Games for all Ages and How to Use Them. (Chicago: TS Denison & Co., 1959).

Wilson, B. O'Brien, M. and Veling,M.Great Gifts Activity Book. (Sydney:Willow Connection, 1998).

Index

55	Whisper, Whisper!	3 years and above.	James 1:19.
56	Bible Whispers	8 years and above.	Luke 8:10.
57	Hear With Your Ears	8 years and above.	Matthew 13:15.
58	The Sensitivity Game	8 years and above.	Luke 8:45.
59	Blind Lead The Blind	8 years and above.	Luke 6:39.
60	Different Points Of View	12 years and above.	1 Corinthians 12:17.

Section 3
Games Based On Bible Knowledge

61	Parable Race	8 years and above.	Matthew 13:13.
62	Advanced Parable Race	8 years and above.	Luke 8:10.
63	Matthew, Mark, Luke And John	8 years and above.	Matthew 4:4.
64	Bible Quotations	8 years and above.	Deuteronomy 31:13.
65	Parable Charades	8 years and above.	Luke 8:10.
66	Proverbs Charades	8 years and above.	Proverbs 16:21.
67	Knowledge Of The Secrets	8 years and above.	Matthew 13:11.
68	Love, Joy, Peace, Patience	8 years and above.	Galatians 5:22-23.
69	Recollections	8 years and above.	Acts 1:1.
70	The Wisdom Of Solomon	10 years and above.	1 Kings 3:9.
71	The Beatitudes	8 years and above.	Matthew 5:3.
72	The Ten Words	3 years and above.	Exodus 20:1.
73	Bible Skips	8 years and above.	Deuteronomy 6:7.
74	Genealogy	8 years and above.	Matthew 1:1.
75	The Twelve Apostles	8 years and above.	Matthew 10:2.

Section 4
Games Based On Parables,
Teachings, Proverbs And Images

76	The The Mustard Seed	3-7 years.	Mark 4:30-32.
77	The Narrow Gate	8 years and above.	Matthew 7:13.
78	Wise Builders, Foolish Builders	3-7 years.	Matthew 7: 24; Luke 6:49.
79	Knock, Knock! Let Me In!	3-7 years.	Matthew 7:7; Luke 11:9-13.
80	Bright Light	3-7 years.	Matthew 5:14.
81	Hidden Treasure	12 years and above.	Matthew 13:44.
82	The Lost Sheep	8-12 years.	Luke 15:4.
83	The Lost Sheep For Juniors	3 years and above.	Matthew 18:14.
84	The Lost Coin	8 years and above.	Luke 15:8.
85	The Lost Coin For Juniors	3-7 years.	Luke 15:9.
86	One Taken, One Left	8 years and above.	Matthew 24:40.
87	Sheep and Goats	8 years and above.	Matthew 25:32.
88	The Judge Said, "No!"	8 years and above.	Luke 18:3.
89	Sheep And Thieves	8 years and above.	John 10:7.
90	The Vine And The Branches	12 years and above.	John 15:5.
91	The Yeast And The Leaven	All ages.	Matthew 13:33.
92	The Net	8 years and above.	Matthew 13:47.
93	Twenty Excuses	8 years and above.	Luke 14:18.
94	Who Is Part of God's Kingdom?	All ages.	Matthew 22:10.
95	Who is Part of God's Kingdom? Variation	All ages.	Matthew 22:10.
96	Parable Board Games	10 years and above.	Mark 4:11.

Section 5
Prayer Games

97	One, Two, Three, Four	6 years and above.	1 Corinthians 1:4.
98	Five, Six, Seven, Eight	6 years and above.	Luke 18:1.
99	Spin The Bottle	6 years and above.	James 5:13.

Section 6
A Game On The Theme Of Justice

| 100 | The Justice Game | 12 years and above. | Micah 4:3. |

Leader's Notes

Leader's Notes